**PRINT CASEBOOKS 8/
THE BEST IN ANNUAL REPORTS**

The Best in Advertising
RC Publications
The Best in Packaging
RC Publications
The Best in Covers & Posters
RC Publications
The Best in Environmental Graphics
RC Publications
The Best in Exhibition Design
RC Publications
The Best in Annual Reports
RC Publications

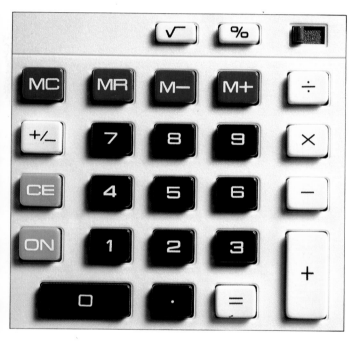

PRINT
CASEBOOKS 8

The Best in Annual Reports

Written by
Rose M. DeNeve

Published by
**RC Publications, Inc.
Bethesda, MD**

Introduction

First published 1989 in the United States of America by
RC Publications, Inc.
6400 Goldsboro Road
Bethesda, MD 20817

Manufactured in Hong Kong
First Printing 1989

PRINT CASEBOOKS 8/THE BEST IN ANNUAL REPORTS (1989-90 EDITION)
Library of Congress Catalog Card Number 75-649581
ISBN 0-915734-58-3

PRINT CASEBOOKS 8 (1989-90 EDITION)
Complete 6-Volume Set
ISBN 0-915734-56-7
3-Volume Set No. 1 ISBN 0-915734-63-X
3-Volume Set No. 2 ISBN 0-915734-64-8

RC PUBLICATIONS
President and Publisher: Howard Cadel
Vice President and Editor: Martin Fox
Creative Director: Andrew P. Kner
Managing Editor: Teresa Reese
Art Director: Thérèse DePrez
Associate Editor: Tom Goss
Editorial Assistant: Susan Scarfe

Fiscal 1986 and 1987, the years covered by this eighth *Annual Reports Casebook*, were a time of unrest for the annual report industry. With other areas in graphic design suffering cutbacks, more designers than ever were vying for position in what they perceived to be a still high-paying business: corporate communications, especially annual report design.

At the same time, the annual report itself was coming under attack. The business media had finally noticed that the annual report industry is big business—around $2 billion per year in the U.S., according to the Wall Street Journal, and $5.1 billion worldwide, according to the New York Times—and articles questioning the role and form of the annual report became more frequent, and often more critical.

One piece appearing in Insight magazine in 1986 reported design fees of $1000 per page, photographers commanding $4500 per day, and illustrators charging up to $10,000 for one painting. Sid Cato's Newsletter on Annual Reports predicted that, with companies spending an average of $500,000 each on their annual reports, the documents would soon be replaced by slick public-relations magazines or videotapes aimed at target audiences. Moreover, by the turn of the century, he ventured, all corporate financial information of the type required by the Securities and Exchange Commission (SEC) will be filed and accessed electronically.

While such threats have been circulating for some time, early in 1987 the SEC issued a ruling that might be interpreted as a step toward making the threats real. In response to a petition filed by General Motors Corporation, the SEC opened the door for the Summary Annual Report (SAR), a condensed, no-frills document with limited financial information, provided that the information be revealed elsewhere, namely in the proxy statement and form 10K. GM had asked for the ruling for the same reasons tendered as complaints in the press—the company felt that annual reports were becoming too complicated, too legalistic and too expensive. For many, the collapse of the "designed" annual report industry seemed imminent.

Yet, to the surprise of the doomsayers and the relief of graphic designers, photographers, printers, and others involved in traditional annual report production, reaction to the SAR ruling was largely negative, especially among securities analysts— those very individuals who had long been supposed to be oblivious to any graphic enhancement of a company's bottom line. A survey released by public-relations giant Hill & Knowlton a few months after the ruling reported that 64 per cent of the analysts interviewed were opposed—some vehemently—to the SAR; clearly, the analysts wanted all of their information in one place. As one respondent put it, "People who won't do a traditional annual report are crazed. They are really showing contempt for the typical shareholder."

Nor did corporations themselves rush to take up the SAR banner, though the reasons for their lack of interest are complex. Big business has always been slow to move away from the accepted way of doing things; but in 1987 there was another reason to avoid making a change of face—the crash of October 19, 1987. Obviously, in the wake of the largest stock market plunge since 1929, a major shift in annual report policy could have sent negative signals to shareholders.

Still, some companies did see Black Monday as an occasion to step back and evaluate their annual reports, and some designers reported sizable cuts in budgets for the 1987 annuals. Budget figures, where available, for the reports shown in this *Casebook* ranged from less than $3 per copy to more than $10, with an average of $5.42—a respectable figure in today's economy. Still, and not surprisingly given recent events, the 600-odd reports reviewed during the *Casebook* judging revealed a largely conservative esthetic.

But there were other factors that resulted in reports which said business as usual. If the drop in stock prices temporarily rocked the executive suite, there were few tremors out in the field, where production by and large continued on course. The crash hit all companies more or less equally and was not precipitated by acts or omissions of any one company's management, or by events in a particular industry—except, of course, the financial services industry. And this industry, as the reports in this *Casebook* will attest, did feel a need to reassure investors and clients of its integrity.

Finally, for those who expected to read in the '87 annual reports explanations of that precipitous event, it should be noted that the annual report has never been the forum for addressing the price of a company's stock, and that in itself would have been reason enough to ignore a crash from which most companies had fairly well recovered by the time their reports were issued.

If there were any trends emerging from among the annual reports entered into this *Casebook* competition, it was a shift in message. Whereas companies used to talk about their management strategies, now the focus is on the solidity of various markets. (After all, even the best of strategies won't help much if no one is interested in buying a company's products or services.) The typical approach to this genre is through the customer testimonial, a device sometimes combined with kudos for the employee or employees who service that particular account. "Market" reports are one big reason for the continuing popularity of people-focused reports, which comprised 40 per cent of this *Casebook*'s winners.

But if *Casebook* jurors were, like most of the entries, a conservative lot, the reports they chose were not wholly without experiment or innovation. Closest to the edge was a report for an entertainment company (Warner Communications), but unusual graphics highlighted other reports in more traditionally conservative businesses (EnergyNorth, Lomas Mortgage Corporation, Metropolitan Chicago YMCA).

In many books, production values made the difference. Indeed, as technical prowess has steadily improved among photographers and printers in the last decade, annual report design has reaped the benefits. Printers, too, are eager to please in order to get a piece of the annual report action. By now, double-saddle-wire binding is the commonplace way to get a mix of papers and surfaces into a smaller report (EnergyNorth, Modulaire); two reports even used a wire-o for the same purpose (Lotus, Burbank Airport). Varnishes were used to heighten certain images as well as to impart tactile qualities in many reports, often with startling effect (Comprehensive Care, Hasbro, Lomas Mortgage). And, by using a number of short, oddly shaped pages cut from what would have been printing waste, one small report got all the bang of a big book (Jay Jacobs).

Photography is, as usual, the number one visualizer in annual reports, with people as the subject of choice. However, the still-life photograph continues to be represented here, both the elegant (Guest Supply) and the avant-garde (EnergyNorth, Eldon). Fully one-third of these pictures were printed in black-and-white, that is, as duo- or tritones of black-and-white images, most often with another color or two added for graphic effect.

Illustration is the prime focus in only five reports (Drexel, Macmillan, Centex, Micom, Burbank Airport) and tends to be representative, if cartoon-like, as opposed to abstract, although most often the subject itself is conceptual. Several entries closed the gap between the two media with photos montaged into illustration, but only one of these made it into this *Casebook* (Warner Communications).

Bringing in this *Casebook*'s Top 30 was no easy task. After the first cut, 45 books remained in the running, i.e., they had been voted for by at least three of the four jurors. During the second round, where jurors traditionally have the option of reviewing all of their choices, some three-vote winners pulled a fourth, while others were dropped from the list. In the end, fully 16 reports received the unanimous approval of the jury—an unheard-of event in a competition where, in other years, the unanimous winners could be counted on the fingers of one hand.

What the jurors saw in all the winners was a strong sense of purpose. "The most common mistake in annual report design is to have more than one idea," juror Colin Forbes observed. "Those ideas begin to battle with one another, and the report gets confused." Added juror Tom Hughes, "The books that don't try to juggle more information than they can handle, or try to say too much, are the most effective." "Our jobs really boil down to making things interesting enough to be read," said juror Douglas Oliver, "and that's where these books really succeed." Summed up juror Robert Newman: "Each of these books has a single point of view and doesn't deviate too far from it. Each sets out to do just enough, and ends up doing it. And that's what makes a strong annual report." —*Rose DeNeve*

Colin Forbes   Tom Hughes   Robert Newman   Douglas Oliver

Colin Forbes, born in London, studied at the Central School of Arts and Crafts. After a period as a freelance designer and lecturer at the Central School, he became an advertising agency art director. He was then appointed head of the Graphic Design Department at the Central School. In 1960, he established his own design practice, having been appointed design consultant to Pirelli in England, and soon afterwards joined with designers Alan Fletcher and Bob Gill to form the partnership of Fletcher/ Forbes/Gill. In the early 1970s, the development and expansion of the partnership resulted in the formation of Pentagram. Forbes moved to New York to establish the Pentagram New York office in 1978. Forbes's work and his contributions to the advancement of the design profession have been recognized with numerous awards and honorary appointments in Europe and the U.S., where he served as national president of the American Institute of Graphic Arts (AIGA) from 1984 to 1986. He was written many magazine articles and is co-author of *Alphabets A-Z, Visual Comparisons* and *A Sign Systems Manual.*

Tom Hughes has worked with three corporations who are known for their corporate identity programs—Polaroid, Apple and Lotus Development Corporation. During roughly five years at Polaroid, Hughes was senior art director for corporate projects. This included the annual report, product introductions and events, and miscellaneous communication projects. In 1982, Hughes was hired by Steve Jobs of Apple Computer as art director for the Macintosh computer project. He was primarily responsible for the introductory Macintosh identity, which has recently been redesigned to greater compatibility with the broader Apple product line. In 1985, Hughes joined Lotus in Cambridge, Massachusetts, where he established the Creative Development Group. The corporate identity program has been completely redesigned under Hughes and all projects from package design to annual report design remain in-house projects. Hughes's studies at several Boston-area academic institutions included majors in English, fine arts, design, museum work, architecture and structural engineering. He worked in various design positions, including art director of the Boston Herald, before joining Polaroid in 1977.

Robert Newman is principal of Newman Design Associates, a design firm specializing in strategic corporate communications. Located in Guilford, Connecticut, the firm lists clients in manufacturing, technology, and financial services, as well as in the arts and human services. Newman is an award-winning designer, with experience in all areas of corporate communications. He has received awards for design excellence from the Mead Annual Report Show, the New York Art Directors Club, the American Institute of Graphic Arts (AIGA), the Society of Publication Designers, the Advertising Club of New York (ANDY), the Society of Typographic Arts, Communication Arts, PRINT's Regional Design Annual and *Print Casebooks*, as well as the *Creativity Annual* for 13 consecutive years. His work has appeared in many design publications, including the German magazine Novum Gebrauchsgraphik and the *Graphis Packaging Design Annual.* He is a graduate of Pratt Institute and has taught Graphic Design and Visual Communications there.

Douglas Oliver is a principal and design director at Morava & Oliver Design Office in Santa Monica, California. He earned degrees from the University of Kansas and Art Center College of Design in Graphics/ Packaging. Upon graduation, in the fall of 1978, he joined Cross Associates in Los Angeles and was soon designing annual reports for St. Regis Paper and Carter Hawley Hale Stores. In 1981, he joined Robert Miles Runyan and Associates, where he continued his annual report work and broadened his experience with major corporate-identity projects and special projects for the 1984 Olympic games. His work has received numerous design awards and has been included in the Mead Annual Report Show, Communication Arts, the AIGA Show, the New York Art Directors Club Show, *Print Casebooks*, STA 100, and the AR 100. His work has recently been selected for inclusion in the permanent design collection of the Library of Congress. His current annual report clients include University of Southern California, Pacific Enterprises, Litton Industries and Pacific Resources.

Casebook Writer

Rose DeNeve

Index

Companies

For many years, Rose DeNeve served on the staff of PRINT magazine. In 1980, she left her position as managing editor there to pursue a freelance writing career. Her articles about graphic design and designers have appeared in PRINT as well as in Graphis and the Journal of the American Institute of Graphic Arts. She has written extensively about corporate communications and is the founding writer/editor of S. D. Warren's *Annual Report Trends*. She also offers general copywriting services, including text for annual reports, from her office in New York City. This is her sixth *Annual Reports Casebook*.

Design Firms
Designers
Art Directors

Photographers
Illustrators

Potlatch

Potlatch reports have become a regular feature of the *Annual Report Casebooks*. Though their history here goes back farther than 1980, the reports since that year have been designed by the San Francisco office of Pentagram Design, formerly Jonson Pedersen Hinrichs & Shakery, and have taken the company from one of the worst periods in the annals of the forest products business to the establishment of Potlatch as an industry leader.

The 1987 Potlatch report, shown here, marks the end of a series. "Instead of taking the long view of the forest products industry each year and talking about the industry as a whole," says Kit Hinrichs, the Pentagram principal who has been the guiding inspiration for the series, "each year we've focused, in depth, on one particular aspect or one particular thing that impacts their business. In this way, we've been able to explain both the industry as a whole and how Potlach fits into it."

Past subjects—"Paper," "The Pine Tree," "Timber Harvesting," among others— have yielded a rich lode of visual materials from which to compile a theme section for the Potlatch report. But this year's presentation was a little different. "The Cooper-Hewitt Museum [the Smithsonian's national museum of design] contacted us to get the Potlatch series for a show they were putting together on annual-report design," says Hinrich. "When Potlatch heard about it, they saw it was a great opportunity to offer some financial underwriting." In fact, the company's involvement

went a bit further—they not only funded the show and the accompanying catalog, but assisted the museum staff in locating both contemporary and historical examples of the form. And Hinrichs himself was instrumental in these efforts.

But if the exhibition was an opportunity to turn something back to the design community that had been specifying Potlatch paper for so many years, it was also an opportunity for the company to associate itself quite openly with that quintessential American business document, the annual report, to which end so much Potlatch product has been dedicated. Hence the decision, at the first meeting between client and designer to discuss Potlatch's 1987 report, that this report would be the last in the current series, and that it would focus on the history of the annual report.

The many outstanding annual reports collected for the Cooper-Hewitt, of course, became the source for the report's visuals, and here one of the challenges must have been, in effect, designing the same book twice—once as the museum's exhibition catalog, and again as the annual report theme section. And in some respects the two designs are similar in both editorial and pictorial content. Both include certain milestone annual reports and archival material of particular importance. Too, both have been designed with the kind of collective exuberance that has typified Hinrich's work for Potlatch in the past—busy, montaged spreads, with both square and vignetted halftones to provide visual interest, and

Using visuals from an exhibition that the company helped to underwrite, the Potlatch annual offers a history of annual reports.

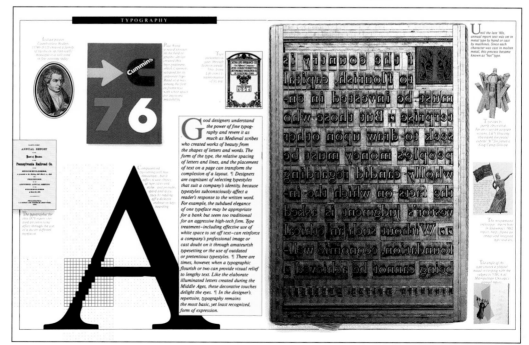

generous use of white space. Still, each book has its own unique character, the museum book being slightly more of a cover-and-spread documentation of the show, and the annual report being a solid member, if the last, of its series.

Like its predecessors, the 1987 Potlatch report relies on a finely ruled grid to hold its disparate textual and pictorial elements. Non-theme pages— the shareholder letter, the operations section, and the financial review—utilize a background of matte gray, with knocked-out headlines and highlight copy, and four-color spot photography and illustration. Once again, Times Roman has been used throughout, and the paper, of course, is all by Potlatch.

It's worth noting here that other series reports have not fared so well as Potlatch's in successive *Casebook* competitions, primarily because their formatting has, in the end, produced a routine report. But while the Potlatch report, especially this series, has to some extent been formatted, its varied and clearly focused subject matter has allowed for endless variation and a kind of vitality perhaps not possible in a formatted report whose theme is always, quite simply, "the company." As the current format expires, one senses that it will be a tough act to follow.

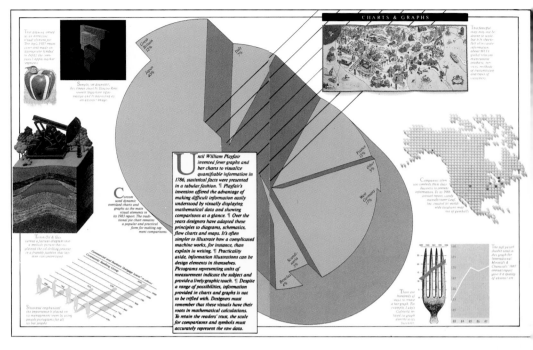

Report: Potlatch Corporation 1987. Tree farming, wood converting, pulp and paper making. 1987 sales $992 million.
Design firm: Pentagram Design, San Francisco
Art director: Kit Hinrichs
Designers: Kit Hinrichs, Lenore Bartz
Photographers: Tom Tracy, Barry Robinson
Illustrators: Doug Smith, Mark Summers, Max Seabough, Dave Stevenson
Copywriter: Delphine Hirasuna
Printer: Anderson Lithograph, Los Angeles
Size: 8½" by 11"; 48 pages plus covers
Quantity: 65,000

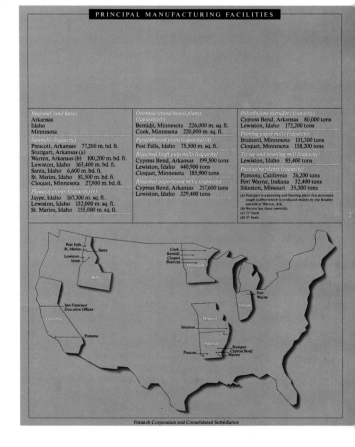

Centex

In its 20 years as a publicly-held corporation and 10 more in private hands, Centex Corporation has built its housing-construction business to position itself as the fourth largest supplier of for-sale housing in the U.S. But the Texas-based company has also diversified its operations, starting with home-building and general contracting, then adding real-estate development and the manufacturing of such construction products as concrete, cement, and gypsum wallboard. In addition, its business has geographically diversified. It was this story of growth and diversification that Centex management sought to reveal in the company's 1988 annual report.

But producing the report brought with it certain limitations. "Due to the nature of the company's business," says Pentagram's Woody Pirtle, art director of the report, "current construction projects change daily. Also, there were no current, quality photographs, and no budget to take them." The solution the designers developed, Pirtle points out, was therefore occasioned as much by the report's low budget as by the need to develop an interesting direction: "We had to be resourceful."

The notion of geography became the focal point. Pirtle and fellow designer Alan Colvin researched commercially produced political maps of the states in which Centex operates and sifted through company files for drawings made by Centex's architectural department. After obtaining permission from the maps' publishers to reproduce them in the report, they

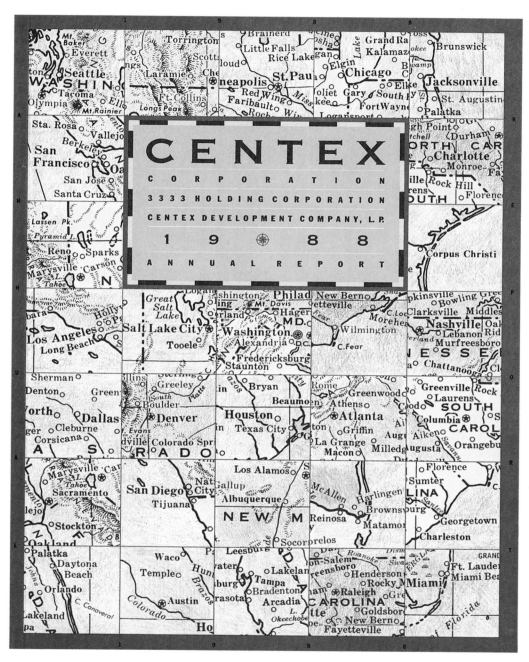

A company's recent geographic diversification is expressed with the clever use of maps.

converted both maps and artwork to line art.

Then came two key decisions in the visualization of the report. "To maintain a consistent style" with these diverse elements, says Pirtle, "we hand-colored them all with colored pencils, using a tissue overlay for separation. Because we were printing very subtle images, we eliminated black from process work and substituted a gray. This gave us a gray for type, and it also helped soften the appearance of the images."

The subtle pencil colorations and the lack of any strong black tones throughout the book, as well as the soft ivory and beige tones of the stock, create an unusually poetic image for a construction-company report. Even simple bar graphs have been drawn with the soft stroke of a pencil, while the gray has been printed as a substantial border around each spread.

But, as is so often the case, it is the handling of a few small details that seals the success of the design approach. In the first instance, graphs and headlines are bordered with the checkered rule so often seen around the edges of a map, or as an indicator in its legend. In the second, a different compass rose has been placed as a signifier at the beginning of each operations section. Finally, a watery blue has been used for map call-outs pinpointing important areas of Centex operation.

HOME BUILDING AND REAL ESTATE

Home building and real estate revenues were $553 million in fiscal 1988, down 7 percent from $592 million in fiscal 1987. Net earnings were $16.3 million, a 48 percent decline from $31.6 million last year. • Home closings in 1988 totaled 5,296 units, an 11 percent decrease from 5,960 units in 1987. The backlog of homes sold but not closed at March 31, 1988 was 1,779 units, 3 percent less than 1,842 units at the same time a year ago. • Revenues from home building and real estate were 38 percent of Centex's total 1988 revenues, compared to 45 percent of corporate revenues in 1987. Net earnings from home building and real estate were 55 percent of the company's 1988 earnings before corporate general expenses and the cumulative effect of an accounting change, versus 65 percent of net earnings last year.

Although an unstable mortgage interest rate environment and the weakened Texas economy combined to depress home closings, revenues and earnings, our home building and real estate operation made significant progress in strengthening its overall positioning. A major step in this geographic diversification program occurred in the third quarter with the acquisition by Centex Real Estate Corporation of the John Crosland Company, an established builder in the high-growth Carolinas. The net assets related to the Crosland purchase were in excess of $60 million. Crosland is the largest home builder in Charlotte, North Carolina and also builds and sells homes in Raleigh/Durham and Wilmington, North Carolina, as well as in the South Carolina cities of Charleston,

Columbia and Myrtle Beach. In addition to its significant and respected presence in these markets, Crosland brought with it an excellent land base and an experienced management team. Crosland is already a major part of Centex's home building business and during the six months after its acquisition generated about 9 percent of our total 1988 closings.

Also in 1988, Centex entered another rapidly-expanding market—San Diego, California—with a start-up operation. We have purchased land there and should begin building and selling homes during fiscal 1989. Including the three new market entries made in 1987—in Jacksonville, Florida, Albuquerque, New Mexico and the Riverside and San Bernardino counties of Southern California—our home building operation has entered a total of ten metropolitan areas during the past two years.

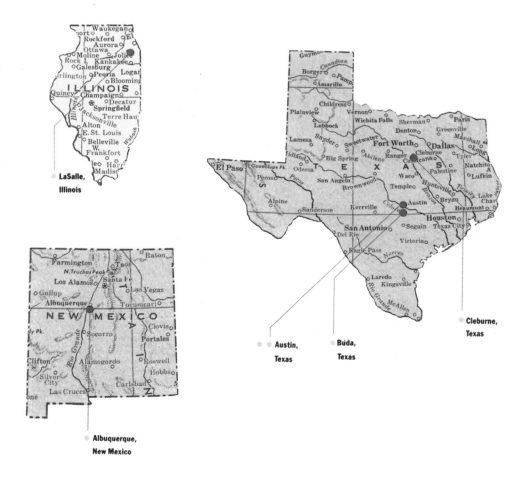

Report: Centex Corporation 1988. Housing, construction and construction products, real estate development. 1988 revenues $1.46 billion.
Design firm: Pentagram Design, New York City
Art director: Woody Pirtle
Designers: Alan Colvin, Woody Pirtle
Photographer: Mike Haynes
Illustrator: Lana Brown
Copywriter: Sheila Gallagher/Centex
Printer: Heritage Press, Dallas, TX
Size: 8½″ by 11″; 50 pages plus covers
Quantity: 30,000

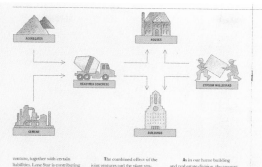

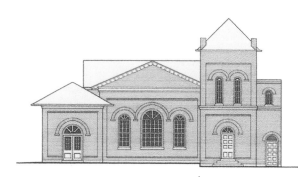

Hand-colored architectural drawings from Centex's files complement similarly colored maps acquired from commercial sources. The maps pinpoint areas of company activity. Various compass roses mark changes of topic in the business review.

The 215-year old walls of Christ Episcopal Church, George Washington's house of worship in Alexandria, Virginia, underwent careful and delicate reconstruction and refurbishing in 1988. The work, which included the construction of a parish house, was performed by Centex subsidiary Eugene Simpson & Brother.

Jay Jacobs

"This job was a big challenge at first," says Luann Bice, one of Hornall Anderson Design Works' three designers on the project, "but in the end, it brought us a great deal of satisfaction." The challenge to Seattle's Hornall Anderson was to design a first annual report for fashion-forward retailer Jay Jacobs, who had just gone public.

The report had to reflect the company's progressive approach to fashion; it had to express its financial performance "in a manner consistent with their style of leadership in the industry"; it had to serve as a capabilities book that would favorably position the retail chain with developers and mall owners as well as stockholders; and it had to do all this for as little money as possible.

As designers of packaging and shopping bags, labels logo, and in-store graphics for the retailer, Hornall Anderson already had a good feel for their client's needs when they began working on the annual report. After initial parameters were discussed with the client, the design team, which included principal Jack Anderson and designer Mary Hermes as well as Luann Bice, tackled the problems of production. "We engineered the project to print on one sheet of paper, using every available space," Anderson says. First, the report was designed to an unusual size—7" by 12"—in order to get the greatest possible number of pages from the sheet. Then, the left-over areas of the sheet were designed and printed in irregular shapes and stitched

Annual

Report

1988

Sales increased 11%, which surpassed the milestone of $100 million.

"Jay Jacobs is emerging as one of the West's leading retailers of junior apparel ...the company has tripled its volume since 1983...and may be going national."

WWD/California
August, 1987

Net Sales (In Millions)

Net Income (In Millions)

Stores in Operation

...stock market crash, the resulting decline in consumer confidence may also have had a major impact.

In spite of general economic reversals which reduced consumer demand, Jay Jacobs' comparable-store retail sales were up slightly for the year. However, the company's overall performance was affected by the disappointing results from the wholesale division.

The principal money-making product of the wholesale division, D.D. Sloane, a sweater, Sansabelt, simply did not sell well during the last part of the year. Sales and profits were on track through August but the usual reorder which were anticipated in the fall did not materialize. The division was left with thousands of sweaters and very few buyers. In order to move excessive inventories, prices were reduced in the third quarter and more dramatically later. This markdown activity led to a fourth quarter pre-tax operating loss of more than $1.6 million for the wholesale division.

Strategic plans have already been put in place to reduce markdowns. At present, inventories for both the wholesale and retail divisions are in excellent condition.

Legend

D.D. Sloane
Wholesale Division

Numerals indicate number of retail stores per state.

A small report relies on ingenious production techniques to create a big impression for a fashion retailer's first annual report.

"Jay Jacobs...targets its consumer base so effectively they've made it a science... They know what the public is buying and what trends are hot."

Harry Bernard, Retail Analyst
January, 1988

We at

Jay Jacobs

are very optimistic

about the coming year.

We remain dedicated to a pat-

tern of controlled, steady growth

and to producing the highest

possible return on in-

vested capital for

our share-

holders...

The company was founded in 1941 by Jay Jacobs, who now serves as Chairman and Chief Executive Officer. During the past five years, the number of stores has doubled and sales have surpassed $100 million.

Several factors have contributed to the company's success: experienced and dynamic merchandisers who utilize a sophisticated data retrieval system to identify emerging fashion trends for a very specific target market; a liberal-return policy; enthusiastic, well-motivated employees; and stores that are geographically well placed in major shopping centers.

As was the case with most specialty apparel retailers, sales in the early part of the year were strong and then gradually weakened as the year progressed. Industry analysts have attributed this slowdown to several factors. First, and most significantly, there was a lack of any clear fashion trends. The weakness of the dollar abroad resulted in higher prices for imported apparel domestically. And, although sales began dropping months before the into the report for unusual effects.

In developing the approach, the design team called in all of the outside people involved in the project—photographer and stylist, illustrator, separator, and printer—for a brainstorming session regarding their respective contributions. From these discussions emerged the one-sheet concept—16 pages, plus a short-page gatefold—wrapped in a text cover. The smaller pages, printed on what would otherwise have been waste, became a diamond-shaped addition to the cover and a highlight table that overlays page one.

The detail work apparent in this report is overwhelming. The book's two fashion spreads were montaged by Wescan, the color separator, in the camera, using commissioned photography, pictures from the client's files, and artwork done on overlays. The commissioned shots, which formed the background of each spread, had to be planned with the final outcome in mind.

"We knew where all the type and photos would occur," Bice says, "and we worked with a transparent grid over the back of the camera and checked everything on Polaroid first." These shots included a subtly patterned backdrop which helped to unify the disparate elements on the spread. Another factor in this regard was the book's carefully developed color scheme, of which the primary components were high shades of pink and blue. These, plus the addition of the gatefold, generate more excitement than one would

think possible in only two theme spreads.

The format continues, unillustrated, into the financial section, where the spatter motif and subtle background pattern continue their unifying effect. The spatters, here as in the front of the report, were created on a film overlay as black line art and then assigned tints in keeping with the report's palette.

Report: Jay Jacobs, Inc. 1988. Retail clothier. 1988 sales $103.7 million.
Design firm: Hornall Anderson Design Works, Seattle
Art directors: Jack Anderson, Luann Bice
Designers: Jack Anderson, Luann Bice, Mary Hermes
Photographers: Kevin Latona/Sylvia South (still life), Philip Dixon (fashion), Dan Lamont (other)
Illustrator: David Bates
Copywriter: John Koval
Printer: Print Northwest, Seattle
Size: 7″ by 12″; 18 pages plus covers
Quantity: 5000

The Burton Group

This report for one of England's premier fashion retailers, designed by London's Michael Peters Literature, appears as a sequel to the previous year's, which was styled much like a fashion magazine. The 1987 edition is a bit larger—what Americans would call "tabloid"-size—and evokes all of the style and excitement of the industry it represents.

But art director/designer David Stocks reports that excitement was not the report's only message of intent. "It had to be coupled with style, confidence, and profitability," he says. "Also, more information had to be more clearly communicated than in previous years."

After an initial briefing, Stocks and fellow designer Nick Austin presented several ideas to their client, who was represented by Guy Salter, executive assistant to the chairman of Burton's. Ultimately, though, the chairman himself—Sir Ralph Halpern—had final approval over the report's design and content.

The ideas represented a range of solutions. One combined five separate brochures in a slipcase. Another, also in two volumes, included a magazine and a more formal accounts statement. And the fourth—the oversized fashion magazine shown here—included an analyst's version that was small enough to fit into a file drawer. Only this last idea was worked into a comprehensive presentation.

"The size was seen as immediately confident," Stocks says. "The accounts were given plenty of space, and the

THE
BURTON
GROUP
PLC

'Successfully
Managing Change'

ANNUAL REPORT 1987

An oversized fashion magazine (11¹¹/₁₆" by 16½") conveys all of this company's style—without sacrificing its businesslike substance.

different sections used different photo and illustration styles to communicate different messages. But we would never have been able to produce the exciting A3 size [297mm by 420mm, or 11¹¹/₁₆″ by 16½″] had we not also produced the A4 version [8 ³/₁₆″ by 11¾″]."

True to the concept, the report's contents are organized in editorial features built around various operating divisions. Photography is variously color or black-and-white and ranges from high-fashion to executive-portrait to environmental. With lots of white space, copy is easy to approach and rewarding to read. And a number of individually styled charts, graphs, call-outs and diagrams quickly inform the reader.

Of particular interest is the cover design—a high-fashion model posed against a slightly out-of-focus wall of black-and-white images. There is a hanging shadow behind the model, and its presence creates a kind of immediacy wholly appropriate to the report's tabloid presentation. "This image was shot with a front-projection system," Stocks says. "The background was produced with Polarpan black-and-white tone film, shot and sandwiched together, then projected."

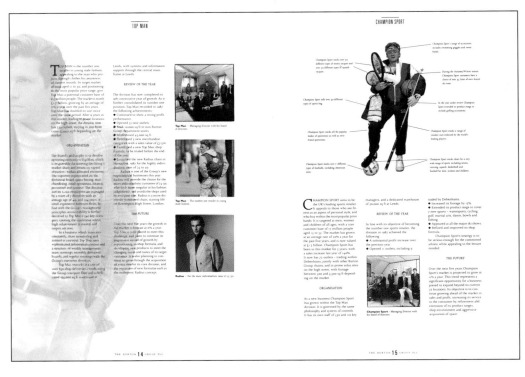

Report: The Burton Group PLC 1987. Fashion and home retailing and related services. 1987 total gross earnings £1.338 billion ($2.395 billion).
Design firm: Michael Peters Literature Ltd., London
Art director: David Stocks
Designers: David Stocks, Nick Austin
Photographers: Chris Simpson, Andy Seymour, David Stewart, Dick Scott Stewart, Simon Warren, John Ross, David Banks
Illustrators: Benoit Jacques, Grundy & Northedge
Copywriter: The Burton Group
Printer: Balding and Mansell Ltd., Cambridgeshire, England
Size: 11¹¹⁄₁₆″ by 16½″ for tabloid, 8³⁄₁₆″ by 11¾″ for analyst's version; 56 pages plus covers
Quantity: 160,000 (both versions)

White space, judiciously applied, is one obvious advantage of the tabloid format. Another is editorial freedom: The reader anticipates that the report's content will take the form of a magazine, and so accepts the variety of visual solutions within.

THE CYCLE OF MERCHANDISING

This report elicited more commentary and discussion from the *Casebook* jurors than any other they reviewed, and with good reason. The book is brashly stylish, and some of the jurors openly wondered whether it had gone too far, whether it had betrayed art for artifice, legibility for style. Yet, perhaps because it appeals to every designer's secret wish to produce a report this daring, they chose to include it in this *Casebook*, both on its own merits and as a milestone of sorts in annual report design.

Warner Communications, Inc. (WCI) reports have been a regular feature of these *Casebooks*. Through the years, their presentation has ranged from simply colorful to splashy showmanship. The 1984 report, however, which appeared in *Casebooks 7*, broke with its predecessors with a format that, like the year's operating results, was somewhat subdued: it was basically a black-and-white book, dashed with two-color highlights.

Since that time, Pentagram Design, producers of the last eight WCI reports, have taken the annual down an increasingly risky road with a collage approach that seems to reach its climax in the book at hand. Having said that, it must also be noted that the report's designer, Harold Burch, states that Warner's 1987 report is not an intentional extension of any series, but a response to the request by his client, WCI chairman Steve Ross, "to capture the high energy of the company's previous two reports."

There was another reason, though, to inject some

Out on the edge: A montage of torn paper, photographs and spattered paint creates a high profile for a major entertainment company.

"high energy"—1987 marked WCI's 25th anniversary as a corporation, as well as 25 years under Ross's stewardship, and the celebration of this dual event became the cornerstone of the report. "We needed," says Burch, "to express Warner's history in a very exciting, energetic way, yet make the company look solid and respectable."

In initial meetings, Burch reports, the client, represented by senior vice-president Geoff Holmes and corporate communications director Les Edwards, wasn't totally sure of what direction to take. Burch's initial idea was to use a photographer and an illustrator working independently of each other, with the illustrator re-interpreting the photographer's pictures. To create comprehensives for this concept, Pentagram flew collage artist John Van Hammersveld to New York to assist in the collaging of some bogus photos. "The style we were proposing was difficult to comp," Burch says, but, by involving the illustrator, "the one solution we presented was very close to the look of the finish."

But when Burch presented the comps, he was told to cut $100,000 from the budget.

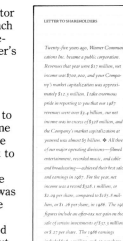

Without sacrificing the integrity of his design, he reduced the album-sized book to one that was only slightly oversized. He also eliminated divider pages, and, instead of mixing papers, put the entire book on one substantial gloss sheet.

After the photographer, Scott Morgan, delivered his commissioned images, which included a portrait of Ross and some symbolic pictures to be used as section openers, Van Hammersveld again flew to New York. This time he worked with Burch and his co-art director, Peter Harrison, to develop the final collages. Client input was important here in terms of assigning priorities to the many photographs that were to be collaged. "Given their history and their success," Burch says, "this was a very difficult task."

One such change involved the cover. "The first cover idea," Burch explains, "was typographical, with 'stars' peering from behind the letters. The politics of who would be on the cover became such a problem that the whole idea was nixed. Bugs Bunny was the only acceptable celebrity, and so we did another idea."

The complete artworks were photographed on 8"-by-10" transparencies, so that, in final

reproduction, they would retain the three-dimensional feeling of their inherent highlights and shadows.

It is these collages that imbue the report with all of the excitement that Ross—and the designers—had hoped for. Reminiscent of a movie-theater wall where a number of posters have been repeatedly put up and torn down, the images combine bits of torn paper, ragged pieces of tape, splatters of paint, standard WCI publicity photos, and/or Morgan's assigned photographs. "Scott's photos act as a foil to all the pick-up images." Burch says, "and bring physical depth as well as current imagery."

While the financial section puts WCI's operating results clearly on the table, this information, too, has been set against jagged color blocks and adorned with rips and tears, all of which give the report a thoroughly cohesive look. But the financial section is also something of a personal triumph for the designers. "Financials have always been a more or less 'sacred' area of annual report design," Burch says. "That's why I think this [treatment] is one of the more important things we've done."

Report: Warner Communications, Inc. 1987. Filmed entertainment, music recording and publishing, publishing and related distribution, broadcast and cable communications. 1987 revenues $3.4 billion.
Design firm: Pentagram Design, New York City
Art directors: Peter Harrison, Harold Burch
Designer: Harold Burch
Photographer: Scott Morgan
Illustrator: John Van Hammersveld
Copywriter: Les Edwards/WCI
Printer: Case-Hoyt, Rochester, NY
Size: 9" by 11⅛"; 56 pages plus covers
Quantity: 115,000

The company that is today Warner Communications publicly traded its stock for the first time on June 19, 1962. Five years later, WCI became involved in the entertainment business when its founder, Steven J. Ross, took the initial steps that ultimately shaped an entertainment industry giant. That year, the company acquired Ashley Famous Agency, Inc., an international talent agency based in Los Angeles, and National Periodical Publications, publisher of DC Comics and Mad magazine. ❖ In 1969, a decisive move was made as the company acquired Warner-Seven Arts, comprised of the Warner Bros. motion picture studio and the Warner Bros., Reprise, and Atlantic record companies. In 1970, Warner Communications Inc. was officially formed. ❖ Over the years, each of WCI's core operations—Filmed Entertainment, Recorded Music, and Cable—has proved to be among the most innovative and profitable in its field.

CONSOLIDATED STATEMENT OF CASH FLOWS

Years ended December 31 (Thousands)	1987	1986	1985
Operating Activities:			
Net income	$328,142	$185,795	$195,305
Adjustments for noncash and nonoperating items:			
Depreciation and amortization	142,424	118,213	23,676
Gain on investments, net	(40,330)	(39,797)	(222,639)
Gain from discontinued operations	—	(22,082)	
Equity-method accounting	24,172	(4,297)	14,046
Changes in related balance sheet accounts:			
Accounts and notes receivable	(159,504)	(66,562)	(156,851)
Inventories	(65,133)	(80,208)	(3,936)
Accounts payable and accrued expenses	189,398	85,771	38,817
Other balance sheet changes	(15,005)	45,317	(25,517)
Excess of provision for income taxes over net payments for income taxes	35,324	61,615	180,191
Cash provided by operations	419,488	283,805	43,992
Investing Activities:			
Capital expenditures	(164,775)	(153,759)	(19,459)
Acquisition of Chappell in 1987 and 50% of Warner Cable in 1986 (a)	(122,839)	(193,050)	
Cash balances of acquired companies	14,793	73,615	—
Proceeds from the sale of MTV and S/TMC	—	326,203	123,852
Proceeds from sale of other investments,			
including investments in operations discontinued in 1984	26,648	122,762	209,535
Decrease (increase) in marketable securities	68,355	(196,996)	(4,202)
Other investments	(39,677)	(6,809)	(30,110)
Cash (used) provided by investing activities	(217,495)	(227,034)	279,616
Financing and Capital Activities:			
Issuance of Series A preferred stock	—	484,402	—
Reduction of debt	(87,129)	(390,749)	(330,091)
Payment of dividends	(91,455)	(48,113)	(7,363)
Other	11,929	17,446	65,818
Cash (used) provided by financing and capital activities	(166,655)	62,986	(271,636)
Increase in cash and cash equivalents	$ 35,338	$119,157	$ 51,972

(a) The principal noncash effects of the 1987 Chappell acquisition on WCI's balance sheet include the following increases in account balances: receivables—$12,813,000; other assets—$270,171,000; accounts payable and accrued expenses—$161,548,000; and, to record the Series A preferred shares issued, shareholders' equity—$577,130,000. The principal noncash effects of the 1986 Amexco transaction include the following increases in account balances: receivables—$167,239,000; property, plant and equipment—$58,920,000; other assets—$132,190,000; long-term debt—$403,213,000; and accounts payable and accrued expenses—$179,966,000; and a reduction in investments of $203,796,000.

See accompanying notes to consolidated financial statements and summary of significant accounting policies.

25

YMCA of Metropolitan Chicago

Samata Associates, of Dundee, Illinois, has been designing annual reports for the YMCA of Metropolitan Chicago for five years. As corporate partners of the Y, and as designers of the Y's fund-raising materials and an internal newsletter, the firm's principals "are strong supporters of the work we do," according to Patrice Boyer, the Y's director of marketing and communications, who oversees production of its annual report.

A slim volume of only 20 pages, the Y's 1987 annual report works in concert with the other printed materials and centers around the client's six core programs. "They have a strategic plan they've been following for the last few years," notes Pat Samata, who art-directed the job, "and they wanted this year's report to shed light on the programs they offer the community." This goal was achieved through the use of unconventional portrait photography, and a layout that works off the letters and numbers "YMCA 87."

In discussions with her partner, Greg Samata, who co-designed the project, a singular solution evolved, one that called for shooting the subjects from an overhead angle that would slightly distort the image. Pat roughed up the idea and presented it to the Y. "This client is very open," she says, "and they loved it."

Working with Patrice Boyer, Samata scheduled photo sessions with community members involved with the featured programs; selections were made to represent both sexes and all ages and nationalities served by the organization. Most of the shots

A limited budget, well spent, creates an involving portrait of an organization's service to its community.

involved only one person, but Samata tells of one portrait—for the community development program—that had six subjects. "We didn't know how we'd pull that off," she says. "One was a doctor who was on call, one was a priest—all were very busy people. But these people were terrific. They all arrived within two minutes of each other; we got them out on the sweep and began shooting. We [Samata and photographer Mark Joseph] were used to shooting CEOs and management people, who don't give you a lot of time. The pose wasn't an easy one, but these people were very patient with us. They were just terrific."

To heighten the angular distortion of the black-and-white portraits, they were set into each squarish spread against one of the jumbo letterforms. Printed in matched tones from a pastel palette, these background forms both ground the vignetted portraits and send them leaping off the page. Body copy, set in a gray borrowed from the photo-duotone and sparked with matching pastel initial caps, was set askew in columns centered line-for-line.

Obviously, an organization like the YMCA of Metropolitan Chicago doesn't have the annual report budget of a corporation. Still, community goodwill can go a long way. "No one makes money on this job," Samata says quite candidly. "But we have a fairly long-standing relationship with this client, and we always try to do something really unusual for them, to make the most out of what limited resources they have."

SPORTS AND RECREATION

he sports and recreation core area encompasses many of our most solidly established and popular programs. It includes all skill development classes, organized sports, unstructured recreational activities and youth resident camping. Within this category we served over 100,000 people last year.

national YMCA standards and backed by training programs such as youth progressive swim and progressive gymnastics have been taking children from fundamentals to mastery for almost 50 years. Our youth resident camps teach a wide range of skills in a setting away from home. They also provide outdoor education to hundreds of school children.

teaching skills, we also organize leagues and tournaments and provide unstructured playing time. Play, according to one source, is whatever you give yourself to completely. The many adults who sort in, pick up basketball games and compete in handball leagues would agree.

we develop standards and improve our offerings, we will pay special attention to 14- to 18-year-olds and those over 55. Since program represents the way the YMCA carries out its mission in the community, we are committed to finding better ways of serving people of all ages.

Report: YMCA of Metropolitan Chicago 1987. Community service. 1987 total assets $59 million.
Design firm: Samata Associates, Dundee, IL
Art director: Pat Samata
Designers: Pat Samata, Greg Samata
Photographer: Mark Joseph
Copywriter: Patrice Boyer/YMCA
Printer: Great Northern Printing, Skokie, IL
Size: 5½" by 11"; 20 pages plus covers
Quantity: 5000

American Express

While most American businesses seemed to bounce back from the stock market's big plunge on October 19, 1987, and did not see fit to mention the event in their annual report, those involved in financial services were more acutely involved, and so may have felt they had some explaining to do. American Express Company is among the latter group, and it addresses its losses at the very top of its 1987 annual report:

". . . 1987 was a year unlike any other in recent history. It was a year the stock market experienced a one-day 508-point plunge, banks added millions to reserves for troubled loans, and changes in ways of doing virtually everything in financial services came fast and furious."

Against this turbulent backdrop, American Express used its 1987 annual report to reassure its shareholders, business associates, and the investment community that this premier purveyor of travel and financial services still had the savvy to manage even these volatile changes.

The main point to communicate, according to Bob Newman, of Newman Design Associates in Guilford, Connecticut, designers of the report, was the company's philosophy in doing business— "the way they evaluate decisions, create products and services, and maintain their leadership position." And the company's complex organization had to be made easily understandable.

In reaching these goals, American Express's director of public relations, Larry Armour,

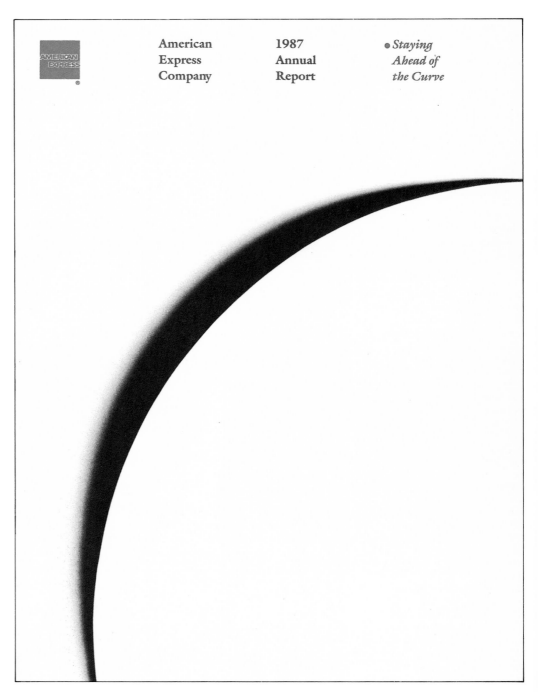

American Express Company

1987 Annual Report

● *Staying Ahead of the Curve*

and project coordinator Janet Lane provided the designers with a theme, "Staying Ahead of the Curve." This catchy phrase, as the report's introductory copy explains, means "being proactive, innovative and entrepreneurial—a leader in everything we do," and Newman's first meeting with his client focused on articulating the theme and defining the overall tone and structure of the document.

While the designers developed several metaphors for the theme statement, one had particular appeal simply because it featured American Express employees. "People are the creators and deliverers of service at American Express," Newman says, "and this is a service-driven company. People are very important to their communications."

The solution also employs a visual metaphor for the slogan—an illuminated curve, such as one might see from a point in space as the sun begins to peep from behind the earth. Although this image—indeed, all of the imagery in the report—is in black-and-white, in the reader's mind it translates immediately into the meaning beyond the metaphor. It does so precisely because it *is* in black-and-white, achieving its power in much the same way as black-and-white movies often create a greater depth and range of meaning than color films do. For this one image, reappearing as it does on the cover and as a backdrop to the employee portraits, unifies the various divisional essays in the report and emphasizes

This report is dedicated to the men and women of American Express whose initiative, creativity and commitment to service and excellence enable us to be— and stay—ahead of the curve.

• Ahead of the pack. State of the art. Cutting edge. There are a lot of ways to put it. At American Express, we say "ahead of the curve." Which, quite simply, means being proactive, innovative and entrepreneurial—a leader in everything we do. It means anticipating customer demands for greater choice in credit cards and devising creative approaches to dealing with the debt burdens of developing nations; providing flawless service face-to-face and unrivaled efficiency in our operating centers; building globe-spanning data networks and creating eye-catching advertising. Being ahead of the curve is the basis for American Express' 137-year history of success and our growing preeminence worldwide in financial and travel services.

After the Crash of '87, a premier financial-services company reassures its customers and shareholders with a subdued annual report.

the company's skilled entrepreneurial management.

The studio photography also allowed certain economies in the book's production. "Personnel outside New York were flown in at less expense than a photographer and an assistant could be flown to them," Newman reports. "As it was, photography was the only item in the budget that we could significantly reduce."

Indeed, a book of this size would seem hard to economize on. Running 78 pages plus covers, and printing half a million copies on web offset, the report had to be designed so as to reduce as far as possible the risk of error. Thus, Newman put the entire report on one uncoated stock, and then printed it with six colors—two for the duotone portraits and four matched colors for graphic effects, one of which was to

Shearson
Lehman
Hutton

Revenues
(Billions of Dollars)

Shearson Lehman Brothers' January 1988 acquisition of The E. F. Hutton Group substantially enlarged the company's retail brokerage network and enhanced its ability to serve clients. The acquisition doubled the size of Shearson Lehman's network to almost 12,000 Financial Consultants in more than 600 offices. The combined firm—Shearson Lehman Hutton—will have capital of approximately $4.2 billion and more than $95 billion in assets under management for others, and will serve some 2.9 million U.S. households.

The unprecedented decline in world equity markets in October and the resulting slowdown in many parts of the investment business took a toll on Shearson Lehman's 1987 operations. The company's revenues for the year were $6.7 billion, unchanged from 1986. Earnings declined 70 percent, to $101 million. American Express' share was $89 million. Strong gains in commission and investment advisory revenues were not enough to offset higher costs and lower revenues from investment banking and market making and principal transactions.

October's dramatic market plunge resulted in an after-tax loss for that month of $72 million, nearly two-thirds of which was a charge related to the underwriting of a British Petroleum equity issue.

Although the Hutton acquisition was the year's most dramatic initiative, Shearson Lehman took other major steps in 1987 to enhance the company's capital and strategic position. In May, American Express Company sold 21 percent of Shearson Lehman Brothers Holdings Inc. common stock to the public while another 9.6 percent was sold by Shearson Lehman to certain of its employees. In April, Nippon Life Insurance Company, Japan's largest insurance company, purchased a 13 percent voting interest in Shearson Lehman. The employee and Nippon transactions increased the firm's total capital by $629 million. Marking this as a true global partnership, Nippon Life now participates in joint ventures with Shearson Lehman and American Express in the United States, the United Kingdom and Japan.

Shearson Lehman's ability to move quickly and decisively, affirmed in October, is due in part to the firm's new data processing facility, the Faulkner Information Services Center. Completed in 1986, the center was designed with state-of-the-art technology to efficiently handle 500-million-share days on the New York Stock Exchange on a sustained basis.

Shearson Lehman is also committed to maintaining exceptionally high-quality personal service. During the market turmoil of October, the firm's offices remained open extra hours, long into the night, affirming the company's commitment to "Financial Consultancy." In the two weeks following the market plunge, new account openings were up nearly 40 percent over the same period in 1986 even though investment activity dropped precipitously.

The firm also achieved major gains during 1987 in its continuing program of quality assurance. Some 65 specific measures were devised to monitor the timeliness and accuracy of a wide variety of client transactions, and a new tracking system was installed to ensure prompt resolution of customer complaints.

Investment Banking: In 1987, Shearson Lehman affirmed its leadership in merger and acquisition and merchant banking activities. Revenues totaled $793 million for the period, compared with $888 million in 1986. Shearson Lehman managed or co-managed 1,143 underwritings worldwide, raising nearly $82.2 billion for corporate and governmental clients, including $1.8 billion for the Community Program Loan Trust, the first-ever public sale of non-recourse government loans.

Internationally, during the year, the firm increased its investment banking presence in Europe and the Pacific Basin. In France, the firm acted as advisor for four major privatization programs. Also, the firm shed new light on the status of international debt by introducing the Developing Country Debt Index—the first gauge to show the market value of bank loans to the largest debtors among developing nations.

Changes in U.S. tax laws and new competition from commercial banks induced a number of investment firms that were once active in public finance to sharply lessen their role. Shearson Lehman, by contrast, affirmed its commitment to this vital marketplace despite the difficult business environment.

Private Client Group: Private Client Group revenues totaled $1.5 billion, up slightly from 1986 levels. In August, Shearson Lehman offered clients shares in the Sector Analysis Portfolio, a mutual fund directed by Executive Vice President Elaine Garzarelli, who for four years has received top honors in quantitative analysis as a member of the *Institutional Investor* All-America Research Team.

Operating Income
(Millions of Dollars)

Total Assets
(Billions of Dollars)

Peter A. Cohen
Chairman and
Chief Executive Officer

26

27

Employees like Maggie Roberts help determine how grant dollars are spent on the local level by serving on philanthropic program committees. Employees also contribute their time, energy and expertise to the organizations we fund.

Maggie Roberts
Special Events Coordinator
Travelers Cheque Operations Center
Travel Related Services

turn the borders of the portrait pages and all of the financials a warm ivory. "We used only one paper and designed accordingly," he explains, "because we knew that the length of the book could change at the last minute. Quantities here were so great that we were afraid extra paper might not be available on short notice." Far from detracting from the report's effectiveness, however, the uncoated sheet adds a certain understated elegance—especially in the photo portraits.

Newman credits his photographer for these distinctive, carefully lit images. "Greg Heisler and I have worked with each other a long time," he says. "I rely on him to translate my direction and trust him to visualize beyond my ability to direct. After all, that's what he does best."

Report: American Express Company 1987. Diversified financial and travel related services. 1987 revenues $17.8 billion.
Design firm: Newman Design Associates, Guilford, CT
Art director: Bob Newman
Designers: Bob Newman, Susan Raymond
Photographer: Gregory Heisler
Copywriters: Larry Armour, Carl Remick/American Express
Printer: George Rice & Sons, Los Angeles
Size: 8" by 11"; 78 pages plus covers
Quantity: 500,000

Comprehensive Care

Comprehensive Care (CompCare) is a nationwide leader in the development, marketing, and management of programs for the treatment of chemical dependencies, including alcohol and drugs, and psychiatric disorders. These programs are administered through the company's own facilities, or through contractual agreements with independent general hospitals.

In 1986, CompCare recorded its first loss in earnings—despite a gain in revenues—in 14 years of otherwise record results. In reporting these facts, management chose a direct editorial approach that made no apologies for its performance, but instead directed itself to the company's strengths.

Among these "positive indicators," as they are called by chairman and president B. Lee Karns, is the company's "winning attitude"—the professional pride and dedication of CompCare's treatment center staffs. And it is through the personal stories of six of these treatment team members, who are fundamental to CompCare's success, that the report hopes to inspire corporate confidence.

Like CompCare's previous report, the 1986 book was designed by the Morava & Oliver Design Office in Santa Monica, California. Also like that earlier report, it relies on testimonials to realize its theme. The visual track here, however, uses an innovative varnish technique that not only heightens the warmth of the employee portraits, but also marks the company itself as something of an innovator.

COMPREHENSIVE CARE CORPORATION · 1986 ANNUAL REPORT

The CompCare Treatment Team:

"Nobody Cares the Way We Do."

A company's winning attitude is exemplified in the dedication of its employees.

At the first meeting with the client, who was represented by CompCare's director of corporate public relations, Ken Estes, the treatment-team theme was approved. Also at that meeting, according to M&O designer Jane Kobayashi Ritch, the decision was made to use full-color photography. Subsequently, Warren Faubel was commissioned to take the pictures.

"I instructed the photographer to shoot flattering, warm portraits," says Ritch. "I wanted to get in close and personal with each one, and I wanted to direct the reader's attention to each person's eyes." At the same time, Ritch wanted to preserve the naturalness of the subject's pose without severely cropping the image.

To achieve these aims, the designer thought of using a matte varnish, tinted with white, to overprint each glossy portrait. With the center of each overprint cut out like a frame, the subject's face emerges as if through a hole in a veil. "The varnish helped direct the reader to the heart of the person," Ritch observes, "yet still let other characteristics show through."

This particular varnish treatment had never been tried before, and Ritch credits both the client and the printer, Lithographix in Los Angeles, with having the forbearance to allow her to pursue the process. "It took some practice press time to perfect it," Ritch says.

To achieve the desired effect, the four-color image was first printed on a glossy stock. Over this was laid a hit of gloss

varnish. Finally came the painstakingly evolved white-tinted, matte varnish. "Timing proved to be critical," Ritch says about the printing process. "We found that if the gloss varnish over the four-color was allowed to dry completely before the matte varnish was applied, the matte varnish would be repelled."

To play off the mixed finish of the photo pages, which allows a bit of gloss to shine through the matte varnish, the designer selected a speckled text sheet with a subtle linen finish—"A nice, warm texture to run opposite the glossy sheet," she says. The text pages were printed in two colors, a warm gray for body copy, and a cool one for headings and captions.

Report: Comprehensive Care Corporation 1986. Treatment programs for chemical dependencies and psychiatric disorders. 1986 revenues $192.9 million.
Design firm: Morava & Oliver Design Office, Santa Monica, CA
Art directors: Douglas Oliver, Emmett Morava
Designer: Jane Kobayashi Ritch
Photographer: Warren Faubel
Copywriter: Ken Estes/CompCare
Printer: Lithographix, Los Angeles
Size: 8½" by 11"; 40 pages plus covers
Quantity: 25,000

Tinted matte varnish adds texture while directing the viewer to the heart of the portrait.

Lotus

Few photographers have shared Bill Gallery's experience of having his photographs determine an entire annual report design effort. But when Lotus Development Corporation's in-house design director, Tom Hughes, began thinking about the company's 1987 annual report, some of his first thoughts were about how to use Gallery's strong, black-and-white portraiture to greatest effect.

As befits a designer at the leading software company, Hughes used a personal computer with a high graphics capability to do his first sketch of the report, and to set up his production schedule. His idea was to have Lotus's president and CEO, Jim Manzi, write a long, signed business review in lieu of the shareholder letter. This review would appear as a running text, into which he would insert case histories of happy customer relationships. The customer stories he saw running on short, square pages that would offer relief from the standard-sized format, which he planned to use horizontally.

With approval from Manzi, Hughes met with Gallery, discussed the report's mood and attitude, and sent the photographer off to Japan, where a major Lotus facility is located, to begin shooting. Hughes also told Gallery to be on the lookout for what he calls "business artifacts"—memos, business cards, invitations—that the designer might be able to montage somehow into the design process.

With his photographer on the road, Hughes and Lotus production manager Nancy Noel began the planning phase. A

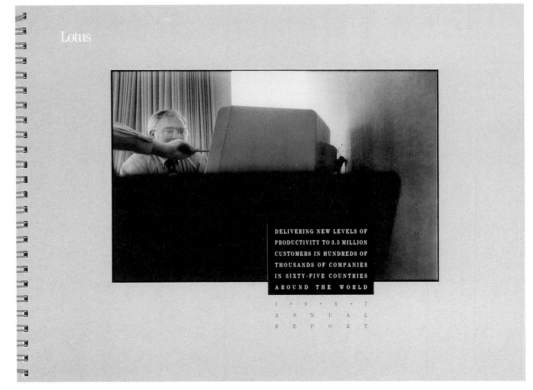

Lotus

DELIVERING NEW LEVELS OF PRODUCTIVITY TO 3.5 MILLION CUSTOMERS IN HUNDREDS OF THOUSANDS OF COMPANIES IN SIXTY-FIVE COUNTRIES AROUND THE WORLD

1 • 9 • 8 • 7 ANNUAL REPORT

Photographic integrity is the mainstay of this report's design, but the wire-o binding allows a mix of papers—and pertinent business cards—to be artfully combined.

critical consideration here was which paper and inks to use to bring off the quality of Gallery's original prints. "Bill's work carries a whole lot of weight," Hughes says, "and we're more interested in protecting it than distracting from it."

Hughes and Noel combed dozens of swatchbooks to compare the white balance of various sheets. Says Noel, "We wanted to match as closely as possible Bill's print papers, and we tried several inks and densities, short- and long-range blacks, until we matched the tones of his prints."

As Hughes envisioned the report, subtle variations in tones would enhance the theme pages by tying together the different elements. He liked the idea of the short portrait page being printed on a gray-flannel text sheet, but that would necessitate laying down a white foil in the image area; another black foil would be needed to run the dropped-out type he wanted up the edge of the page. Clearly, this wasn't feasible.

"Flannel is not the type of sheet where you can really simulate a glossy photograph," Noel says; "it's just not the same. So we opted to reproduce the flannel in color and hoped some of the texture and look of the sheet would come across. And then we could also have the photos at their highest quality."

Thus, coated papers in two shades of white were selected on the basis of the photography. The first, a cooler white, was used for the "flannel" sheet and major portraiture. In order to put the type along the edge and avoid an expensive die-cutting bill, the designers printed on one side, scored and folded the sheet at the proper place, and went to a wire-o binding to accommodate it. (The budget also allowed for Hughes to print the flannel texture inside the folded sheets, for those who like to pry open such things, but he decided they really didn't need to do that.) The photographs on these pages were printed as cool black-and-white tritones. The rest of the theme section was put on a warmer white coated stock. The smaller shots of Lotus employees, who were involved in the stories of the customer portrayed in the larger photographs, were printed in warmer tritones on this white sheet. The gray used here, though not the same as the matched color used to create the flannel, is a good complement. "We had to maintain a fine balance," Hughes says. "It could have looked really bad if the colors weren't in synch."

From the "artifacts" that photographer Gallery had collected, Hughes opted to use only the business cards from the people photographed. These were reproduced, complete with embossing and thermography, on a standard card stock and then glued back-to-back with a business card from the Lotus employee. Hughes was amused by the implication Lotus people were backing up their customers.

The book went to bed in the dead of winter, and to avoid their precious mechanicals being lost or delayed in a predicted blizzard, Hughes and Noel flew to Cincinnati, location of the printer, with their drawing boards and did the boards in a hotel room. Gallery later joined them at the printer for a press check. Finally, 10-times-66,000 business cards were die-cut, glued together in pairs, and hand-collated with the rest of the theme section.

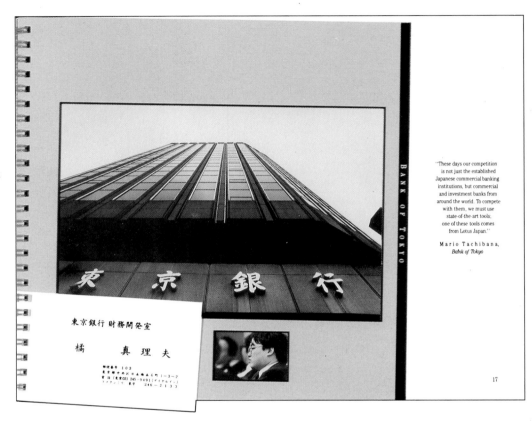

"These days our competition is not just the established Japanese commercial banking institutions, but commercial and investment banks from around the world. To compete with them, we must use state-of-the-art tools; one of these tools comes from Lotus Japan."

Mario Tachibana,
Bank of Tokyo

Report: Lotus Development Corporation 1987. Development, production, and marketing of application software and information services. 1987 sales $395.6 million.
Design firm: Lotus Creative Development, Cambridge, MA
Art director: Tom Hughes
Designers: Tom Hughes, Nancy Noel
Photographer: Bill Gallery
Copywriters: Jim Manzi, Tom Lewis/Lotus
Printer: The Hennegan Co., Cincinnati, OH
Size: 11″ by 8½″; 46 pages plus covers
Quantity: 66,000

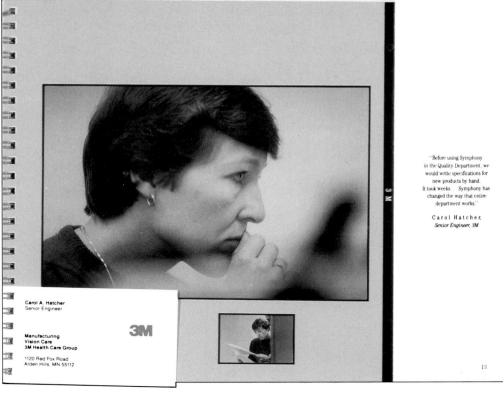

"Before using Symphony in the Quality Department, we would write specifications for new products by hand. It took weeks. Symphony has changed the way that entire department works."

Carol Hatcher,
Senior Engineer, 3M

H.J. Heinz

Annual reports from H. J. Heinz are consistent winners in *Casebook* competitions, yet there is nothing consistent about their style or execution, except that they are consistently excellent. The report shown here was produced by the same basic client/designer team that has produced all of these previous *Casebook* winners—in fact, all of Heinz's reports for the last 12 years.

In fiscal 1987, the idea was to present a series of reports within the annual report, and so the letter to shareholders, the yearly review, and an unusual collection of "field reports" (whose titles were engraved in a non-metallic gold on the report's red cover) were assembled in typographically similar presentations. What differentiates one from the other are two things, the one subtle—a change in paper stock—and the other profound—the use of striking black-and-white portraiture. The former incorporates a soft gray text sheet for the so-called field reports, which were written and signed by Heinz executives worldwide, and the letter, which is a kind of field report for the whole company, written by Anthony J.F. O'Reilly, chairman, president, and CEO of Heinz. In each case, the businesslike essay has been signed in a different color ink. The other paper—a premium coated sheet with a fine gloss—is used for the operations text (the one more or less impersonal report) and to print the portraits which interleave the field reports.

It is the portraits that make this book strong, eye-catching,

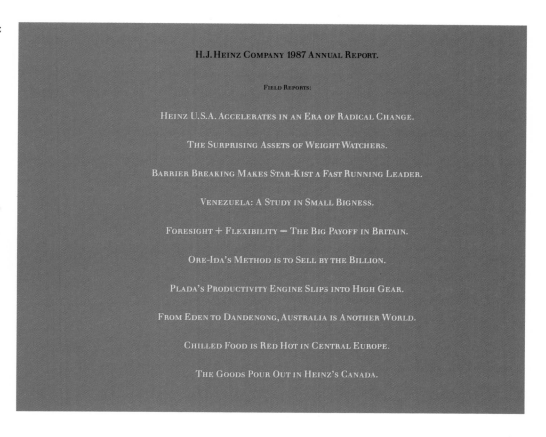

H.J. HEINZ COMPANY 1987 ANNUAL REPORT.

FIELD REPORTS:

HEINZ U.S.A. ACCELERATES IN AN ERA OF RADICAL CHANGE.

THE SURPRISING ASSETS OF WEIGHT WATCHERS.

BARRIER BREAKING MAKES STAR-KIST A FAST RUNNING LEADER.

VENEZUELA: A STUDY IN SMALL BIGNESS.

FORESIGHT + FLEXIBILITY = THE BIG PAYOFF IN BRITAIN.

ORE-IDA'S METHOD IS TO SELL BY THE BILLION.

PLADA'S PRODUCTIVITY ENGINE SLIPS INTO HIGH GEAR.

FROM EDEN TO DANDENONG, AUSTRALIA IS ANOTHER WORLD.

CHILLED FOOD IS RED HOT IN CENTRAL EUROPE.

THE GOODS POUR OUT IN HEINZ'S CANADA.

Elegant vellum engraving of late Heinz chairman, Henry Heinz II, appears on flyleaf.

Unusual executive portraiture gains strength in a black-and-white presentation.

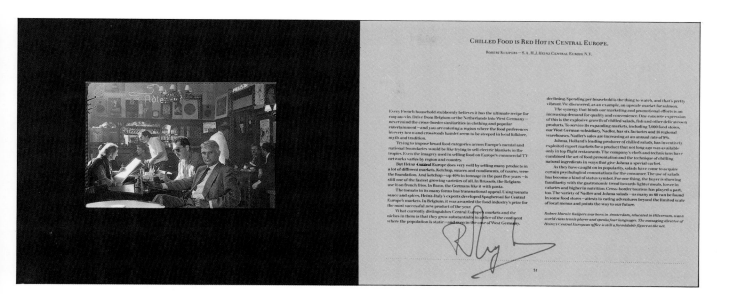

and truly unique. Following a time-honored practice in producing Heinz reports, Bennett Robinson, chairman of Corporate Graphics, Inc., in New York, retained a photographer experienced at portraits but not with working in the "commercial" arena. "Rodney Smith is really from the gallery world," Robinson notes. "He seems to get this wonderful seriousness in his portraits, yet they're not somber. They capture an authoritative intent of purpose. These people look like exactly what they are—managers of a world-class company."

The success of the portraits seems to lie in the fact that Smith has been able to get his subjects out of their suits (several, including the chairman/president/CEO, appear in their shirtsleeves) and into some fairly unique environments: The managing director of the company's Central European office is seated in a pub with a beer in his hand; his counterpart in Italy is photographed from behind on a narrow, brick-paved street; the head man himself is aboard an airliner, where he leans pensively into a window. The portraits were printed in gloss inks and framed in a dull black matte, which makes them fairly leap out at the viewer.

There was one other unusual point about this report, and that was a vellum engraving of Henry J. Heinz II that appeared as a flyleaf inside the front cover. Heinz, descendant and namesake of the company's founder, died in February 1987, after 56 years of service to Heinz. The shimmering flyleaf, with its ghosting of the brief tribute on the following page, is an elegant memorial to the man who, for three generations of Heinz employees, provided the connecting link with the company's origins.

Report: H.J. Heinz 1987. Food and food processing. 1987 sales $4.6 billion.
Design firm: Corporate Graphics, Inc., New York City
Art director: Bennett Robinson
Designers: Bennett Robinson, Erika Segal
Photographer: Rodney Smith
Illustrator: Rosemary Webber.
Copywriter: Tom O'Hanlon
Printer: Anderson Lithograph, Los Angeles
Size: 8½" by 11"; 56 pages plus covers
Quantity: 150,000

For some time, MONY Financial Services had been using the word "enterprise" to characterize its operations in insurance, investments, and other financial services. When the company, represented by director of public relations Larry Clark and project coordinator Suzanne Platenic, called in Newman Design Associates to design their 1987 annual report, the word had already been expanded into a theme, "The Spirit of Enterprise."

" 'Spirit' was a way of defining the company's culture and approach to doing business," says the report's art director and chief designer, Bob Newman. " 'The Spirit of Enterprise' was both for internal motivation and explanation and for external communication. The company had changed from its traditional businesses, and this had to be made clear."

Since the company is not public but owned by its policyholders, the report had to communicate to them as well as to people in the business community. Its theme, therefore, was particularly suited to the report's marketing responsibilities.

This was Newman's first report for MONY, so it was vital that he quickly grasp his client's needs. "My contacts at MONY were encouraging and enthusiastic, very decisive and intuitive," he says. "Both Larry Clark and Suzanne Platenic were good at giving direction, that is, at defining their message and establishing the look, feel, and positioning of the report vis-á-vis other companies in their business."

Integral to the solution was the word "Spirit" itself, which was embossed on the front cover and printed in varnish across the muted stripes on page one. Each of the five letters in the word was made to stand for one corporate characteristic—Service, Performance, Innovation, Respect for the Individual, Integrity, and Teamwork. These attributes were in turn defined and expanded in the report through a mission statement for each, a portrait and a case history involving both customers and employees, and additional customer stories that elaborated on the attributes.

At the heart of the report, however, are the warm, black-and-white full-page portraits by Bard Martin. "Bard is great at getting a personal and accessible moment in the subject he shoots," Newman says, "without making them do anything out of their own character." To facilitate color control, the only black inks used in the report were in photo tritones, where they could be manipulated without altering the color of the type.

Typography throughout the report is Bodoni, chosen, Newman says, because it's "classic, elegant, and timeless," and Helvetica Condensed, "to add some contemporary typographic elements." The palette for the three PMS tones is subdued—a shadowy blue-green and salmon-pink that complement a solid "corporate" gray. Making for a nice continuity, these shades are used variously for the "stripes" on page one, along the edges of the portraits, and in blocks of

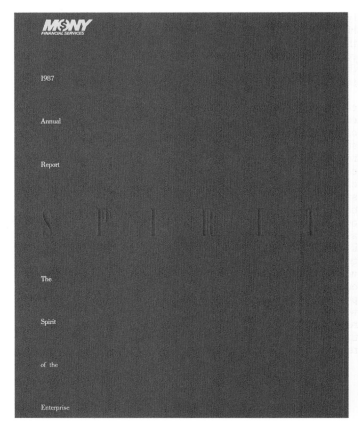

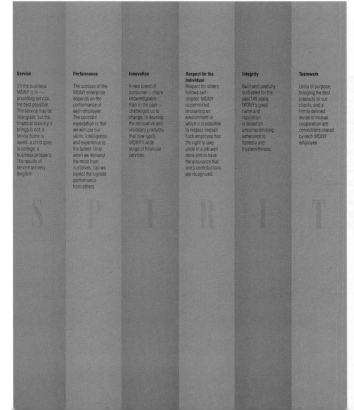

type contrasting with the deep blue-gray type used throughout the portrait pages. Conversely, coated and text papers in different colors were used to segregate its various parts.

Newman feels that, especially considering it was the first time out with this client, the spirit of teamwork was particularly strong in producing this report. "As designers, we are constantly reminded that we cannot do our work alone," he says. "Supportive, intuitive clients who motivate us to do our best work are as necessary as the photographers, illustrators, printers, and typographers that collaborate with us. It was a brave step for our contacts at MONY to produce this document, as it was very different from past reports. For us, it was one of the most successful 'first' reports we have ever done."

Houston-based North American Mortgage Company, specialists in residential loans, reacted swiftly to customer needs when the Texas economy experienced a sharp downturn. This MONY subsidiary renegotiated thousands of loans for homeowners who were unable to meet monthly payments. Through quick action, the company's mortgage professionals prevented numerous foreclosures. Caught in the midst of this sudden decline were Anna Doneson, a registered nurse, and her young son Douglas (photo left). With her income cut, mortgage payments became a heavy burden and Anna feared losing their home. The company, realizing her predicament, was able to modify her loan to an adjustable rate, with substantially reduced mortgage payments. Still a proud homeowner, Anna credits North American with a thoughtful and realistic solution to her problem.

In a competitive world filled with deadlines, the ability to meet and surpass client expectations is increasingly rare.

For more than 30 years, the Association Plans department of Group and Pension Operations has delivered service of the highest caliber and offered quality life and health insurance products to association clients. Association Plans' reputation for service, plus affordable rates and a network of experienced field underwriters near military bases, was the reason the Military Benefit Association selected MONY to underwrite group life insurance for its 73,000 members.

A new service-oriented product developed by Group, MONYFlex, enables clients to offer employees a variety of benefit choices, including multiple option medical plans and reimbursement accounts for health expenditures with tax benefits.

Providing innovative financial products and meeting the highest standards of service in today's marketplace are major components of the MONY success story.

*S*ervice

Dr. Eric Ornella, a MONY policyholder, suffered a spinal cord injury that left his legs paralyzed. John E. Sargent, MONY's rehabilitation director, helped the Cincinnati orthodontist design an office with total wheelchair accessibility. Within two years of his accident, the doctor had resumed his practice.

With the MONY Market Account, life insurance beneficiaries may choose to receive policy proceeds through an interest-bearing account instead of in a lump sum. This enables them to write checks to cover immediate needs during a difficult and confusing period and is an example of MONY service at its best.

Each month the Planner Services department of Financial Service Corporation answers 1,000 technical inquiries on investment products and financial planning. This gives the representatives serviced by the department a true competitive edge.

Evaluation Associates, Incorporated (EAI), a rapidly expanding MONY subsidiary, counsels over 50 large retirement and endowment fund clients with aggregate assets of over $40 billion. Additionally, EAI structures investment funds, currently exceeding $2 billion, for bank clients and fund sponsors.

Appealing customer portraits and an unusual palette enhance an editorial theme called "Spirit."

Report: MONY Financial Services 1987. Insurance, investments and other financial services. 1987 assets $15.9 billion.
Design firm: Newman Design Associates, Guilford, CT
Art director: Bob Newman
Designers: Bob Newman, Katrina Hinsch
Photographer: Bard Martin
Copywriter: Suzanne Platenic/MONY Financial Services
Printer: W.E. Andrews, Redford, MA
Size: 9″ by 12″; 40 pages plus covers
Quantity: 60,000

Talent, remarkable achievement and a firmly rooted sense of what's most important are just some of the outstanding personal qualities of Raymond C. Veselik, CLU, ChFC (left). Selected by a committee of his peers as MONY's Man of the Year in 1985, Ray, general manager of MONY's Itasca, Illinois agency, exemplifies the highest contributions to his industry, community and family. With 3,000 clients, a wife and eight children and numerous civic responsibilities, Ray, who's won every major MONY sales award, has an attitude of concern and admirable. When Kent Campbell, a sales manager who works for Ray, experienced the death of his brother and then the loss of his home in a fire, Ray was always there with support. Way beyond what most employees could expect from a boss, Ray's actions illustrate his number one priority: the welfare of those around him.

Every company, no matter how large or small, must count individual members as its most valuable asset. How those members are viewed by the employer—and how they view themselves and their peers—influences their personal and business behavior.

MONY recognizes that the human spirit responds to encouragement, and that people do their best work when they are personally fulfilled. Charities or non-profit organizations to which MONY sector employees have donated significant time are given cash awards by VIM (Volunteer Incentive at MONY). Additional program incentives intended to recognize performance, achievement and loyalty are tailored to each sector or subsidiary.

Respect also means concern. MONY's corporate conscience expresses itself through a variety of grants and programs with a philanthropic theme of 'Family.' Help was given to children, the elderly, the homeless and hungry, those with acute illnesses and others. Employees at North American Mortgage Company pitched in on two Saturdays to paint and repair four houses belonging to elderly or disabled homeowners.

Respect. It has to be earned, nurtured and sustained. At MONY, each person contributes to the strength of the enterprise.

*R*espect for the Individual

Guest Supply

Weary travelers know these products well. When, at the end of a tiring day of meetings and missed connections, they check into an upscale hotel, they find a range of "amenities" in the bath to help them clean up and calm down.

For 18 of the country's top 25 lodging chains, these personal-care items are provided by Guest Supply. Indeed, Guest Supply was one of the first companies in the guest-amenities business and is considered a leading marketer and manufacturer in the field. In addition to products developed and packaged in its own facilities, Guest Supply maintains exclusive rights to market certain nationally known brands to its lodging and travel-industry customers.

In 1986, Cook and Shanosky Associates, of Princeton, New Jersey, were charged with designing and producing Guest Supply's first "designed" annual report (previous ones had been produced in-house by the company's packaging design team). "Our target message," says Don Shanosky, who, together with his partner, Roger Cook, designed the report, "was that Guest Supply is a leader in a business that not too many people realize exists. We wanted to convey this by establishing the feeling of elegance associated with the hotels themselves."

The cover of the report immediately sets the tone—a proprietary brand, in a house-designed bottle, lies with a single blue iris against a rich marble background. The marble, Shanosky reports, came from a local marble importer's showroom, where

GUEST SUPPLY, INC.

1986

ANNUAL REPORT

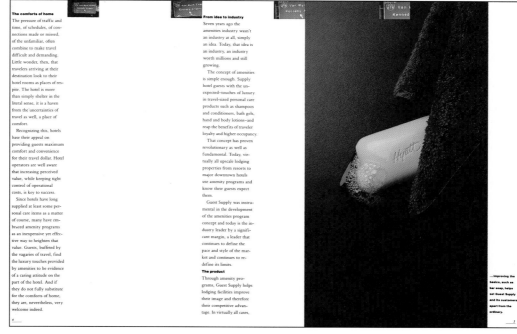

the designers searched through stacks of samples to find the one with just the right subtleties of grain.

Inside, the copy—which was also the responsibility of the design firm—was set in narrow columns with lots of white space between. Major photography took the form of still lifes of proprietary or licensed products, this time set against dark gray backgrounds. "The marble on the cover set up the luxury-amenities theme," Shanosky comments, "but we felt it would be too much to continue it through the whole report." The neutral backgrounds also precluded having to deal with "decorating" each shot to resemble this or that hotel room. In keeping with this premise, additional props were selected with an eye for their dark color, which, of course, serves to play up the products even more.

But after the luxury theme came another message, and its implementation gives this report a unique twist. In the words of Shanosky, "We wanted to remind the reader of what travel is really like— rushing to the airport, getting a cab, being stuck in traffic—and to suggest how rewarding a hot bath can be." This point was made through a series of animated insets that wend their way through different areas of each spread. The sequences capture the kind of frenetic pace pursued by the modern business traveler, the disjointed life of fleeting road signs and ticking clocks. Their intrusion on the otherwise controlled layouts makes for graphic counterpoint to the soothing comforts pictured in the larger still lifes. "These shots help to establish what amenities really mean," Shanosky says. "In this business, travelers have grown to expect these little luxuries, and the better hotels are aware of this." With this carefully executed report, Guest Suppy convincingly presents itself as a prime factor in making these hotels attractive and comfortable places to stay.

Report: Guest Supply, Inc. 1986. Personal-care items for the travel and lodging industry. 1986 sales $33 million.
Design firm: Cook and Shanosky Associates, Inc., Princeton, NJ
Art directors/designers: Roger Cook, Don Shanosky
Photographers: Arthur Beck (still lifes), Paul Kopelow (insets), Tom Graves (executive portrait)
Copywriter: Gerald F. Reimel
Printer: Stephenson, Inc., Alexandria, VA
Size: 8½" by 11"; 24 pages plus covers
Quantity: 25,000

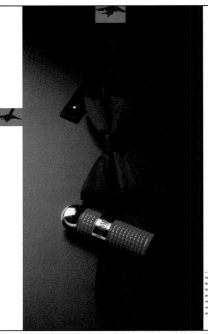

minded traveler, recognizes the added value amenity programs bring but must fulfill that need at low unit cost. For these facilities, Guest Supply offers generic amenity programs that provide quality products at a modest unit cost.

While these programs typically contain fewer personal care items than custom programs, they fulfill the hotels' needs by surpassing guests' expectations.

The company
Guest Supply is a vertically integrated company offering concept development, product design, manufacturing, packaging and distribution of personal care products. By operating as an integrated single source of supply, Guest Supply offers its customers timely response to their needs and minimizes delivered cost.

Over the past year, Guest Supply manufacturing facilities have been both expanded and improved. New high-speed filling equipment has increased processing capacity, while an expanded quality control laboratory has allowed product monitoring to keep pace with the plant's higher output. Plans for 1987 include the manufacture of soap, allowing

Guest Supply to further control its own cost.

The expansion of the manufacturing arm of Guest Supply has allowed the order/delivery cycle to be shortened considerably. Parallel improvements in data processing and computer capacity have increased the speed of order processing. In a complementary move, Guest Supply has also expanded its telecommunications center to handle the ever increasing number of customer inquiries and orders.

The management team
In a young company in an equally young industry, the issue of depth of management and succession planning must be addressed. Consequently, we are pleased to report that during the year Guest Supply was successful in attracting additional top-caliber talent to the company.

These additions have provided further management depth to the company. Equally important, the company now has a broader base of executive experience on which to draw in order to manage and direct its future growth. During 1987, the company plans to concentrate its human resource efforts on improving middle management.

...top flight hotels look to Guest Supply for distinctive proprietary packaging that reflect the style and image of their property...

Tiny photographs that recreate the hectic pace of the business traveler contrast serene product still lifes for this purveyor of upscale hotel "amenities."

Eldon Industries

When Jane Kobayashi Ritch, of the Morava & Oliver Design Office in Santa Monica, California, began work on Eldon Industries' 1987 annual report, she was a bit stumped: for the second year in a row, Eldon management had chosen the same editorial theme—"Growth By Design." "We needed to show 16 years of growth in a new way," she explains, "and to integrate the idea that the design philosophy of the company was the reason for the growth."

At the first meeting with the client, who was represented by marketing vice-president Harold J. Fatt, the theme was presented and a decision was reached to photograph Eldon office products in a "high design/high fashion" style.

"We found the perfect photographer to shoot the products," Ritch says. "Stuart Watson was able to add his style to the shots and make the products seem like 'art pieces.' He gave us wonderful shots to work with."

In an inspired solution, Ritch combined the graphs—which plainly point up Eldon's growth—with the photographs, die-cutting the bar charts and laying them over the photography. "The die-cuts were an exciting way to highlight the 16 years of growth in an unusual and eye-catching manner," she says. "And I also felt this was a great way to show the basic philosophy of the company—that great design and growth work hand-in-hand."

But the die-cuts themselves took some time to develop. Since the photography was to print on a glossy sheet and the type on matte, Ritch originally tried to die-cut the charts from a matte sheet that had been printed solid black. "We did a test run," she says, "but when we die-cut the charts, the white edges showed through."

Next, she tried an all-black uncoated sheet with a fine linen texture, but new problems arose. "We had to estimate which weight would work best," she says. "The paper had to be heavy enough to withstand all the die-cutting. Unfortunately, we were limited to the heaviest book weight, which we felt was too light for the cuts, and the lightest cover weight. Of course, the ideal would have been something in between."

Ultimately, the designers went with the cover weight. To key each bar in the graph, the printer made two hits of tightly registered white.

The placement of the bars in the chart had also to be considered in designing the photography. "We had to make sure shadows and dark areas did not fall in key areas of the die-cuts—like at the top of a bar," Ritch says. "We had to keep shifting lighting around and overall keep the photos 'high key.'" The results, surprisingly, were not limited in any way. Indeed, Watson seems to have been urged forward by the limitations of his assignment: his minimalist constructions, assembled from variously textured building materials and selected Eldon desktop accessories, really do set these basically utilitarian objects apart.

One other problem, however, arose during the cover development. Originally, it, too, was to have been die-cut to reveal the theme phrase,

which was printed on page one. Since the cut was obviously a difficult one to register in the bindery, the designers opted to print the die area black instead, and let the reader's eye fill in the blank as the report is opened.

Finally, in keeping with the book's slightly vertical format, Futura Condensed was used throughout. "The whole book took on a vertical characteristic," Ritch says. "It was 1″ deeper than usual, and had the vertical bar charts highlighted. I thought the condensed face appropriate." So did the *Casebook* jurors.

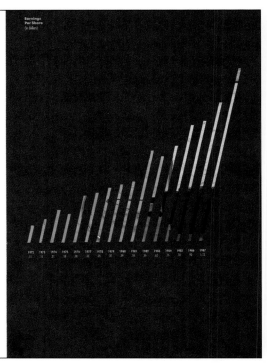

Charts, die-cut from cover-weight text paper, overlay full-frame product photography conceived as fine art.

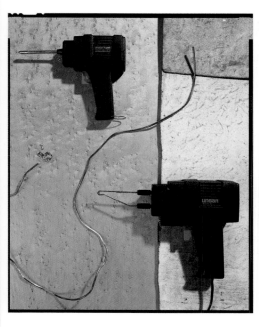

Report: Eldon Industries, Inc. 1987. Office products; production tools for the electronics industry. 1987 sales $84 million.
Design firm: Morava & Oliver Design Office, Santa Monica, CA
Art directors: Douglas Oliver, Emmett Morava
Designer: Jane Kobayashi Ritch
Photographer: Stuart Watson
Copywriter: Harold J. Fatt/Eldon Industries
Printer: Lithographix, Los Angeles
Size: 8½″ by 12″; 40 pages plus covers
Quantity: 7000

Nichols Institute

The Nichols Institute is a small, for-profit medical research corporation that translates its findings into specialized testing services for diagnostic, prognostic, and therapeutic use by physicians and hospitals. Designed by Jim Berté, of Robert Miles Runyan & Associates in Playa del Rey, California, the Institute's 1987 report is an apt reflection of the company's technological prowess—and in no way reveals the difficulties that transpired during its production.

"At our first meeting with the client," Berté says, "the chairman was quite clear in how he saw his company, and what its goals were. He also told us that he wanted a beautiful book, and that he was very open to an imaginative solution."

Berté first proposed an oversized book measuring roughly 9″ by 18″ and featuring large, full-page photograms made with a process that Berté and photographer Scott Morgan had been developing for some time. These prints, which montaged assorted medical paraphernalia like syringes, test tubes, and skeletal structures into sepia-toned artwork, were to run full-page opposite a running text highlighted by small portraits of members of the Institute's staff. Because of their experimental nature and their extremely large size, the photograms created a powerful, if unusual, visual theme.

Then, several days before the job was to be delivered to the printer, the Institute's chairman changed his mind. The oversize format, and the large photograms, made him uncomfortable, and he asked

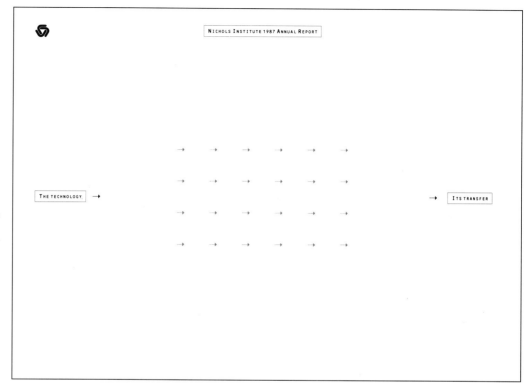

the designers to come up with another solution. Berté had about three days to redesign the report.

Berté immediately reset all the copy so as to fit within a more traditional 8½″ by 11″ horizontal format. With the photograms scrapped, the 4″-by-5″, black-and-white Polaroid portraits became the design's focal point. To add texture and visual interest, they were scanned with their gooey-looking borders intact; the portraits themselves were printed as duotones, while the borders were separated for four-color process. "Some of these images, as pure portraiture, were a little unusual in their posing," Berté says, "but fortunately, the chairman loved them."

The type—a high-tech-looking face called Optical Character Recognition B—was printed in gray for the running text and in a shaded purple for the brief, boxed case studies of Institute technology that had been transferred to its testing services. The type is cool and technocratic and the perfect foil for the warmth and messiness of the portraits. Says Berté, "The type is bizarre-looking and, I thought, well suited to the kind of business the Institute is in. They get all kinds of print-outs and statistical data from the tests they run, and the type has the feeling of this kind of information."

Berté reports that the chairman of the Institute still wasn't completely satisfied with the design, but that there simply was no time left for further refinement if they were to meet their press window and make the scheduled delivery

Williams Jones, MD

The technology

Genetic amniocentesis allows physicians to detect certain chromosomal abnormalities before the birth of a child. Such abnormalities can result in birth defects, such as Down's Syndrome. Before the development of this technology in the early 1970s, there were no means for gaining such information prior to delivery. Making such information available to assist in the care of patients is the goal of diagnostic research. In most amniocentesis cases, women enjoy the reassurance that no chromosomal abnormality exists during pregnancy. Although it cannot rule out all potential birth defects, genetic amniocentesis goes a long way toward managing those abnormalities which have a significant relationship to maternal age.

Its transfer

Developing and building a department of skilled technologists to handle the intricacies of technology such as genetic amniocentesis forms the core of my work. As a Scientific Director, I seek out individuals whose experience and sensitivity make them adept at the very close, labor-intensive detection process that can find chromosomal abnormalities in human genes. It is painstaking and delicate work.

Dr. Jones maintains an intimate link with our day-to-day work. He reviews every patient case, and when urgency dictates, he calls to discuss results with the client. Fully one third of our caseload reflect genetic abnormalities which must be addressed with sensitivity. Quality control is the most critical component of this process to ensure the accuracy of our findings. When dealing with the quality of human life, nothing less would be acceptable.

Professor of Medicine and Pediatrics
Director, Division of Medical Genetics
University of California, San Diego
Department of Medicine.

High-tech type contrasts the hands-on look of the Polaroid process for this data-based medical research corporation.

date. Nonetheless, the designer made the best of a ticklish situation: the report has brought him some professional recognition as well as personal satisfaction. That he was able to "save" the report at the last minute was particularly gratifying. "I think it's a good book," he says, "even in its diluted form."

Report: Nichols Institute 1987. Medical research and testing. 1987 revenues $55 million.
Design firm: Robert Miles Runyan & Associates, Playa del Rey, CA
Art director/designer: Jim Berté
Photographer: Scott Morgan
Copywriter: Julie Suhr/Robert Miles Runyan & Associates
Printer: Ralph's Printing, Los Angeles
Size: 11″ by 8½″; 40 pages plus covers
Quantity: 20,000

Polaroid

Most designers would shudder at having to design an annual report using photography supplied by the client. But when that client is the Polaroid Corporation, the shudder is one of pure delight.

Designed by Michael Benes and Varus Artinian, of Benes Communications in Waltham, Massachusetts, Polaroid's 1986 report is the third in a series employing a similar graphic treatment and color palette, using Polaroid picture formats and solid-color backgrounds as an integral part of the design. But the 1986 report is especially successful, in the words of Michael Benes, at "making instant photography exciting once again."

As designers of all of Polaroid's financial and consumer literature, Benes Communications already had a good understanding of the client when they began to think about the 1986 annual report. Foremost in their minds were two points Polaroid wanted to convey: that there are many varied uses for Polaroid films, and that there are many different Polaroid film types. In addition, the client wanted the report's design to suggest that "in every scene, everywhere you look, there are opportunities for a Polaroid picture."

This last point became the peg on which the report's overall design was hung. Various Polaroid prints, culled from the client's files, evoked a multiplicity of picture-taking occasions—on safari in Africa, at the swimming pool, on a rainy day, on vacation in the Tropics, in front of the CRT. The shots were also selected to

Polaroid Corporation 1986 Annual Report

The subject is Polaroid's instant photography. The excitement inherent in its immediacy is well described by the upbeat illustration and high-color palette used in this report.

represent various Polaroid formats, from the square and slightly horizontal frames of consumer instant-picture systems to black-and-white and professional films.

The photos themselves are for the most part so strong that the designers could have left well enough alone. Instead, they placed each one more or less in the center of the page and then, in bold crayon strokes, the image was completed with a drawing extending out to the paper's edge. In every case, the drawing and the page background were kept in the pure bright tones of the original Polaroid print. Because of budget restrictions, the drawing and background colors were matched to PMS shades using standard four-color process. Finally, leaving no base uncovered, the designers posted shots of Polaroid's many products, again photographed with Polaroid equipment, throughout the financial section. Typography was Helvetica Condensed, in deference to Polaroid's corporate style, but also because of its contemporary, high-tech connotations.

This report, Benes tells us, was particularly well received, both by younger Polaroid employees and by senior management, who tend to be more conservative in their views. "This latter was surprising," he adds, "considering the report's avant-garde design."

But management's instincts were quite correct: subsequent feedback told Polaroid's corporate communicators that the report appealed equally to

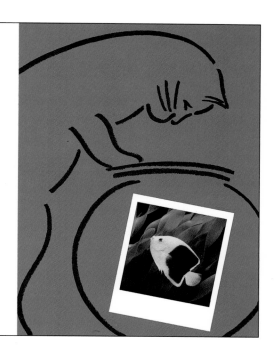

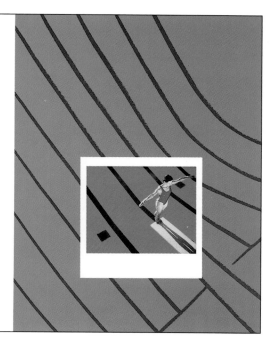

younger and older members of the company's target audience of investors and shareholders. As a result, the design concept was extended to a new packaging and product program.

Report: Polaroid Corporation 1986. Instant imaging systems. 1986 sales $1.6 billion.
Design firm: Benes Communications, Waltham, MA
Art director: Michael Benes
Designers: Michael Benes, Vartus Artinian
Photographers: Various
Illustrators: Lark Carrier, Jamie Hogan, Marie McGinley
Copywriter: Gordon Lewis
Printer: Acme Printing, Wilmington, MA
Size: 8½″ by 11″; 40 pages plus covers
Quantity: 100,000

Required product photography is couched in the company's own 35mm materials.

Annual Reports/52

Lomas Mortgage
Corporation

In every *Casebook* edition, there has been one or more annual reports from the Lomas & Nettleton Financial Corporation or its subsidiaries. These award-winners always come out of the same design firm—Richards Brock Miller Mitchell, in Dallas—and always strike a theme close to the American heart.

The annual report presented here, for the Lomas Mortgage Corporation (LMC), is no exception. Founded in 1985 to finance single-family residential properties, LMC in 1987 posted a gross income of $91 million, with assets above the billion-dollar mark. The annual report for this year focuses on the recipients of much of this home-buying assistance—the children of the post-World War II Baby Boom.

"The message here was to affirm the company's stature as a lending institution helping the Baby Boom generation attain upscale housing," says Brian Boyd, who designed the report. "They are now reaching the age where their earning power is the strongest, and we wanted to illustrate this strength and the impact this generation has had on America."

And, one could add, on the American landscape. Immediately upon opening the report, the reader is faced with a gatefold displaying a vast tract of frame housing, some of which appears to be occupied, and some of which is still under construction. From the looks of the automobiles in this photo, it was taken in the early 1950s, at the height of the Boom, and is meant to illustrate the introductory text that runs on the folded-in part of

LOMAS MORTGAGE CORPORATION ANNUAL REPORT 1987

Where it began: The postwar Baby Boom that has resulted in the current demand for housing is represented by an archival photograph, die-cut and mounted on the cover.

the gatefold: "Racing to meet demand, builders and developers tried new, faster means of construction to frame endless rows of standardized tract houses. Educators pushed for bigger school buildings and revolutionary teaching methods to handle larger classes . . . this great wave of children heightened our perception of the possible. No one in America today would think of building, of living, as people did before the Boom."

The colors here are a bit murky, and not with entirely pleasant effect, for the picture, after all, represents what LHC's clientele are fleeing. At the peak of their earning power, the copy reminds us, the Baby Boomers are now acquiring houses larger than those of their parents, more substantial homes that reflect their greater expectations. Truly, this report is an homage to a generation, pieced together with fabric from the lives of five individuals who were part of the Boom, either as a parent

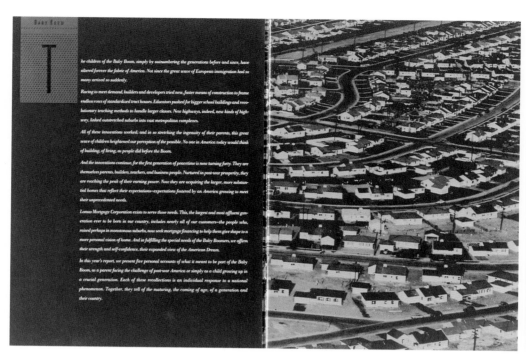

Inside the report, a gatefold describes the unimaginativeness of tract housing, and Lomas customers reveal their desire for something better.

"facing the challenge of post-war America or simply as a child growing up in a crucial generation."

The theme section, which contains the personal accounts of these individuals, runs entirely between the chairman's letter, which, as in other reports within the L&N family, is also the operations review, and the financial section that starts on page 16. These verbal and visual portraits are designed for maximum appeal, sitting as they do within entirely black pages, like photos in a family album. Continuing the historical feel of the cover photo, which is a vintage shot of a USO couple embracing on a dance floor, each spread contains a historical photograph of the subject as well as an artful, commissioned portrait by photographer Greg Booth. Each of the subjects has some connection with a burgeoning population searching for places to live, to work, and to educate its children.

Type here has been run in the burnished bronze of the opening photo, kept legible by wide leading and tightly registered printing. The deckled edges of the smaller photographs, formed by dropping their white borders out of the background, adds to the believability of the report's premise that these people, themselves the products of "monotonous suburbs," now have a greater and more personal vision of "home," which reflects their generation's expanded view of the American Dream. By helping them realize that dream, Lomas Mortgage Corporation positions itself here as an integral and dynamic force in the building of America.

JOHN FREEMAN IN ONE OF THE NEW CUSTOM-BUILT HOMES HE'S PUTTING UP IN DALLAS

JOHN, AGE 5, AT HIS FAVORITE OAK; ABOVE HIM, HIS FIRST TREEHOUSE

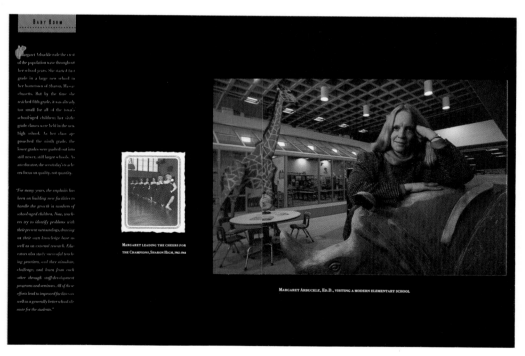

MARGARET LEADING THE CHEERS FOR THE CHAMPIONS, SHARON HIGH, 1962-1964

MARGARET ARBUCKLE, ED.D., VISITING A MODERN ELEMENTARY SCHOOL

Report: Lomas Mortgage Corporation 1987. Mortgage lender. 1987 revenues $91 million.
Design firm: Richards Brock Miller Mitchell and Associates, Dallas, TX
Art director/designer: Brian Boyd
Photographer: Greg Booth
Copywriter: Kevin Orlin Johnson/ RBMM
Printer: Heritage Press, Dallas, TX
Size: 8½" by 11"; 32 pages plus covers
Quantity: 30,000

Pacific Resources

An independent energy company based in Honolulu, Pacific Resources, Inc. (PRI), operates in Hawaii, California and Texas, as well as in the South Pacific, Singapore, and Hong Kong. It was this presence on the Pacific Rim, as well as its management strength, that PRI sought to emphasize in the company's 1986 annual report.

For designer Douglas Oliver, of the Morava & Oliver Design Office in Santa Monica, California, the solution revolved around separating the operations portion of the theme from the management portion. The two-pronged approach could have been distracting, but through careful selection of photography, color palette, and layout proportions, he managed to find a place for everything and to put everything in its proper place.

The initial meeting with the client brought together the designer and PRI vice president for corporate communications Andrea L. Simpson, who was also the report's copywriter. At that time, the theme was broadly discussed, along with possible solutions. However, in the end, only one solution was presented to the client, and it received complete approval. Given what Oliver calls "tight budget constraints requiring close monitoring of specifications and alterations," it was to his advantage that his client asked for no changes.

Oliver's solution operated on two highly dissimilar yet parallel tracks. The one engaging the operations photography was designed boldly, with dramatic, horizontal duotones representing key areas of

Pacific Resources, Inc.

1986 Annual Report

Handsome black-and-white location photography unifies a report built on both operations and management strengths.

PRI's activities. Framed in the glossy white borders of its own spread, each photograph works with its brief caption to both command the reader's attention and convey the subliminal message of strength.

On spreads alternating with the operations photos is PRI's management story. Here, the glossy sheet has been overprinted with a buff-tone matte ink. Against this neutral background, type is run in taupe and a deep, reddish brown. The only sparkle on the page is to be found in the small black-and-white manager portrait that is tucked to one side. These spreads transmit a feeling of order, strategy, careful control—and suggest that PRI managers also share these attributes.

In keeping with the feeling of restraint, a page of simple pie charts faces the opening of the financial section. The financial statements themselves were organized simply on an ivory text sheet and printed in the same taupe and brown tones used in the operations pages.

Report: Pacific Resources, Inc. 1986. Gas and oil trading, and marketing. 1986 revenues $816 million.
Design firm: Morava & Oliver Design Office, Santa Monica, CA
Art director/designer: Douglas Oliver
Photographer: Rick Golt
Copywriter: Andrea Simpson/PRI
Printer: Anderson Lithograph, Los Angeles
Size: 8½" by 11"; 52 pages plus covers
Quantity: 25,000

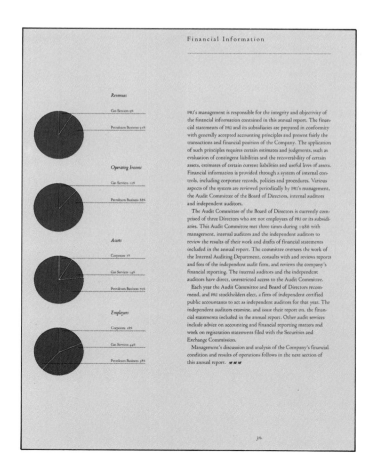

Macmillan

Information is the basic component of all of Macmillan's businesses, which include publishing, instruction and home-learning, and information services. But it's this last business which in 1986 showed outstanding performance, and which the company sees as a major player in its future success.

"Macmillan's previous reports had relied on photography," says Kent Hunter of Gips + Balkind + Associates, designer of the report, "and had focused on one division within the company with a kind of report-within-a-report. But, though they're known for their publishing, information services is where they're heading. It's a direction that's going to be very profitable for them, and this is what we wanted to stress in this year's annual report."

But how best to express that promise? "I wanted the book to be a classy publishing book, but still show that they're high-tech," Hunter continues. "And I definitely didn't want to use photographs of people working at computers. It seemed like a good opportunity to work with illustration."

Hunter reviewed a number of portfolios before he settled on Mark Penberthy. "Though Mark hadn't done so many corporate things," Hunter says, "he had done a number of editorial illustrations for business publications, and his work was rich and dense with color."

It's this very richness, keyed by Penberthy's lush oil paintings, that creates the mood for this report. Though their subject matter is information

M
ACMILLAN, INC.

Information

is changing the future

of business...now.

1986 Annual Report

A business built on information highlights information services as the key to its future success.

LEXANDER POPE noted, "A little learning is a dangerous thing." But in the early eighteenth century, when Pope was writing, a little was all the formal knowledge most people could hope to achieve. Few could read or write, and fewer still could afford to own a book.

Today, depending on one's point of view, we live at a time of information abundance . . . or glut. Much has been written about the sudden growth of information, its importance in today's advanced economies, and the new business opportunities it presents. The information explosion is changing our lives. Is it, as many contend, the social revolution of our century?

Not really. If there is an "information revolution," it began before computers . . . even before Alexander Pope. It began perhaps 550 years ago, when a master printer named Johann Gutenberg first used movable, cast letterforms to print a book. And it spread 100 years ago, when Ottmar Mergenthaler's magnificent contraption—the Linotype® machine—automated the typesetting process. These were the innovations that started to make more information available to more people, creating the modern publishing industry and beginning information's upward spiral.

EMERGENCE OF
THE INFORMATION
SERVICES GROUP

AT MACMILLAN, information services is a business separate from publishing and includes more than just print materials. But our experience in publishing deepens and shapes our view of information. Macmillan has been in the publishing business since 1869. We have grown by contributing to the world's information, knowledge, and understanding. All three of our core businesses—Educational Publishing, Information Services, and Instruction—begin with information and add value to it for our customers.

In the Information Services Group, we draw upon Macmillan's publishing heritage to meet the most modern of needs: for information to be gathered, selected, interpreted, and presented in a way that is helpful to customers . . . turning potential glut into useful abundance for decision-makers, professionals, and scholars. Whether the product is a single journal or a multivolume reference with thousands of pages, it must have this dimension—information with value added—to be produced by Macmillan's Information Services Group.

During the past five years, the sales and operating income from Macmillan's information

How much is an answer worth?

Sifting through extraneous infor-

mation can be expensive . . . and

wasteful. When information is

accessible, when its format is easily

manipulated, it ceases to be a burden—

and becomes a powerful tool.

[6]   [7]

1986 SALES
BY BUSINESS SEGMENT

Publishing   46.6%

Information Services   22.3%

Instruction   19.6%

Home Learning and
Reference Materials   5.7%

Gump's   5.8%

technology, and they are tied to editorial points provided by the client, the artworks themselves are anything but "high-tech" in character. Rather, by building up his canvases with layers of paint, gesso, and varnishes, Penberthy has managed to soften the subject of cold, hard facts. The result is a warmly elegant book that avoids visual cliché.

To complement the paintings, Hunter chose the pattern of a marbled endpaper as a decorative border for each spread and to line the back cover. "This paper comes out of the tradition of publishing," he says, "and its color and texture worked well with Mark's paintings. Its decorative look also provided a subtle contrast with the high-tech subject matter." Highlight shades of ocher and blue-green were built from process colors, and the whole book was printed on a luxury creme-colored sheet.

"Over the years, we have continued to reposition our client as their corporate strategy has developed," comments David E. Anderson, who managed the project for GBA. "This report was a major step away from the product-oriented, photographic books Macmillan has historically produced, and its contrast of an elegant, traditional design with a high-tech, forward-thinking message, we feel, creates a simple yet powerful annual report." We couldn't have said it better.

Report: Macmillan, Inc. 1986. Publishing, instruction, information services. 1986 sales $817.8 million.
Design firm: Gips + Balkind + Associates/The GBA Group, New York City
Art directors: Phil Gips, Kent Hunter
Designer: Kent Hunter
Illustrator: Mark Penberthy
Copywriter: Michael Clive/GBA
Printer: L.P. Thebault, Parsippany, NJ
Size: 8½″ by 11½″; 44 pages plus covers
Quantity: 45,000

How much is enough? How much is too much? A rising tide of facts can overwhelm the user—unless usability and efficiency are planned into the medium itself.

[19]

The link between publishing and high-tech information processing is forged with lush conceptual illustration.

MICOM Systems

MICOM, as a manufacturer of data communications products, is one of the many companies that have suffered because of recent trends in the data communications market. First, the development and mass availability of the personal computer disrupted the mainframe and microcomputer world; then, a great deal of confusion arose over how to network these different technologies. Finally, in the wake of the AT&T break-up, an increasingly complicated set of choices, proffered by newly independent and competing telephone companies, further confused the data communications marketplace.

It was obvious that these industry-wide difficulties had to be addressed in MICOM's 1986 annual report. But how? At his first meeting with his client to discuss their annual report, Douglas Joseph, of Robert Miles Runyan & Associates in Playa del Rey, California, suggested that MICOM "use illustration to solve the problem of visually depicting intangible subjects"—namely, those problems facing the industry, and MICOM's reponse to them. "The illustrations allowed them to talk about things that could not be photographed," says Joseph, "like choices and solutions."

With approval from his client, who was represented by manager of investor relations Joanne Martz and corporate communications specialist Karen Winner, Joseph commissioned a set of illustrations. "The original illustrator I selected did very editorial, pen-and-ink drawings," he says, "the type you see in the opinion section of the newspaper. His work was the sort that combined human and animal elements to create satirical characters." After seeing the first roughs, however, the client asked for "someone with a lighter attitude."

At this point, Joseph called illustrator Guy Billout. "Billout is one of a handful of illustrators who, to me, renders ideas instead of just pretty pictures," Joseph says. "He thinks like a designer, not like an illustrator." Moreover, he felt that Billout's ironic sense would be a good follow-up to the photographs used in the previous year's report, each of which, he says, had some kind of visual twist. Joseph showed Billout's portfolio to MICOM's president and got an immediate green light.

Billout, who works in New York, was provided with lines from a state-of-the-industry essay to illustrate. "We discussed possibilities over the phone," the designer says, "and then he air-expressed sketches for me to present to the client."

Billout's drawings were given extra punch by printing them in dull fluorescent process inks on a dull creme stock, which was also hit with a dull varnish. The drawings were then interleaved with the industry essay, which was printed on a satiny white sheet. The gray type and bright orange "blips" used to signify each new paragraph link together text and illustrated pages.

In addition, a four-page question-and-answer section was placed between the essay and the financial review to explain how MICOM's many

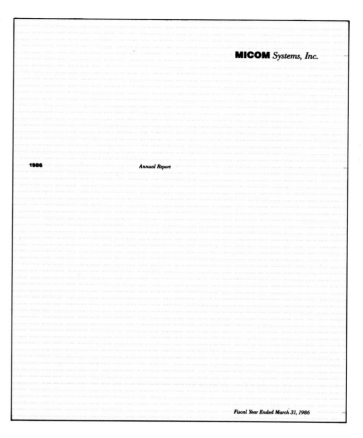

Choices

Choices

complex

Choices   *Choices for the average customer are more* *today, and this has inevitably*   *delayed*

Choices   *a number of decisions for purchasing*

                         data communications equipment.

The theme of our annual report a few years ago was "Growing up with MICOM," and the cover depicted a ten-year-old taking measure of his height. Three years have passed since that picture was taken, and the young company represented has begun to mature. The same might be said of the data communications industry at large: we are young adults now. The passage has not been without the turmoil of adolescence, but the transition has tempered us, as it often does, and experience has added new dimensions to our perspective. As grownups, we must cope with new challenges and influences. We must modify and adapt to a dynamic marketplace as never before. —— Those of you who have been following our progress for the past few years will recognize that making adjustments to a changing marketplace is standard practice for MICOM. It is the hallmark of our company to be alert for approaching opportunity, and this year has been no different. We are still probing the data communications marketplace for new targets, exploring possibilities for innovative products to exploit market niches others have ignored, and modifying our current strategies and products as our customers' requirements change. —— What is different is the condition of the data communications market itself. Several events of the last few years have registered an impact on the computer world far more profound than most forecasters expected. For many companies in the information processing and data communications fields, the effect was severely damaging – for some, devastating. All were sobered by the sudden downturn, for the first time

adjusting and then readjusting to slower product demand. —— Before reviewing industry factors that influenced the data communications market, we'd like you to know what kind of company MICOM is, what it does, and how it operates. These three elements are basic to understanding how we arrived at our position in the market today, but more significantly, they will illustrate why MICOM is so well positioned to respond to future market directions.

Who We Are MICOM makes and sells data communications equipment, the gadgets and systems that enable computers and terminals to "talk" with one another. With MICOM products, information generated by computers can be used by peripheral devices like printers and terminals, or these devices may feed data into the computer. This data flow might travel just a few feet or several thousand miles, and the number of interacting devices can range from two

to a few to thousands. The data communications equipment itself can be as simple as a cable connector or as complex as a complete networking system. We make "widgets" selling for a few dollars and sophisticated products costing many thousands. In all, MICOM sells more than 600 data communications products. —— It's important to remember that MICOM does not make computers or the terminal equipment driven by them. What it does make is the transmission equipment in between. That includes products like statistical multiplexors, data PABXs or switches, line drivers and modems, protocol converters, local area networks and many other products needed to get data smoothly, quickly and correctly from source to destination. —— MICOM develops and markets devices for which a market already exists or can quickly be developed, devices that enhance the performance of computing equipment already in place. Our solutions are quick to install and easy to use, with rapid payback to our customers. We take the mystery out of data communications and the technical hassle out of installing remote or local applications.

Ironic illustrations, printed in dull fluorescent inks, play within a restrained graphic format in this report for a manufacturer of data communications products.

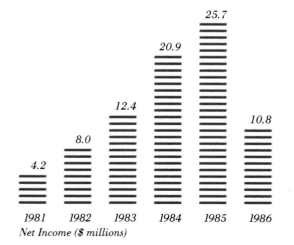

25.7

20.9

12.4

8.0

4.2

10.8

1981 1982 1983 1984 1985 1986

Net Income ($ millions)

esoteric, "black-box" products boost the power of computers and data processors. The products themselves are illustrated with schematic diagrams, which relate nicely to the quotes that Billout has illustrated, both in their placement on the page and in their airy, poetic visual treatment.

"The people at MICOM are among those rare clients who have an understanding of how design functions and solves problems," Joseph says. "In the two years I worked with them, I was given an unusual amount of latitude to pursue non-traditional directions. I attribute much of our joint success to the client's willingness not to be driven by literal images of people and products."

Report: MICOM Systems, Inc. 1986. Data communications products. 1986 sales $189.5 million.
Design firm: Robert Miles Runyan & Associates, Playa del Rey, CA
Art director: Robert Miles Runyan
Designer: Douglas Joseph
Photographer: Steven Rothfeld
Illustrator: Guy Billout
Copywriter: MICOM
Printer: Lithographix, Los Angeles
Size: 8½" by 11"; 44 pages plus covers
Quantity: 25,000

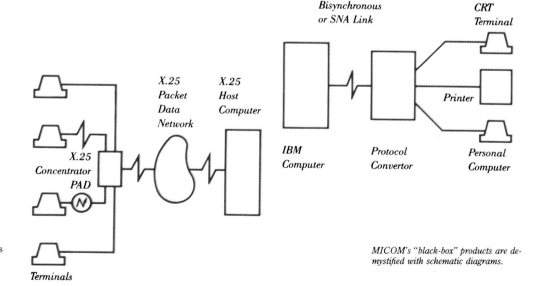

MICOM's "black-box" products are demystified with schematic diagrams.

Toronto-Dominion Bank

This, the Toronto-Dominion Bank's 1987 annual report, is its 132nd, and the 11th in a series produced by Toronto designers Eskind Waddell to position their client as an industry leader. In 1987, the report was also conceived to convey that "Toronto-Dominion is customer-responsive," says art director Roslyn Eskind, "innovative and flexible in meeting changing needs, and concerned with human needs."

Through informal discussions that preceded the first meeting with the client, Eskind and report designer Peter Scott had come to grasp their client's special objectives for the 1987 report, and so were able to bring to that initial encounter several verbal ideas. One of these—to present banking concepts through illustrations that would be run in combination with photos of bank representatives and clients—was especially well-received. "Susan Stein, the bank's assistant general manager, and Linda Binns, their publications manager, were wholly supportive of our unorthodox concept," Eskind says, "despite the fact that banking is a conservative industry. They helped us with our research and provided reference for the illustrations."

With eight months to complete the project, Eskind Waddell had adequate opportunity for planning and development. Still, as Eskind points out, early planning and production meetings were critical to the design approach, in which soft crayon drawings seem to float over and around the severely horizontal "black-and-white" portraits.

THE TORONTO-DOMINION BANK

132nd Annual Report 1987

• TD became the first Canadian bank to purchase seats on the Toronto, Montreal, Vancouver and Alberta stock exchanges, which improved access to the exchanges' automated trading systems for GLIS customers and expedited the execution process.

• Green Line Investor Centres, based on the successful design of our Toronto Investor Centre, will open in Montreal and Vancouver early in 1988, providing sales offices for retail and institutional customers.

Commercial Customers

Canada's booming commercial sector is creating new demands for financial services. Meeting the banking needs of small and medium-sized businesses requires an understanding of the pressures and challenges facing the entrepreneur.

Commercial customers want two things from bankers: quality of and continuity in the management of their accounts. Given the importance of the commercial account manager, Toronto Dominion has established training programs that emphasize account management skills and provide a firm grasp of business principles as well as product knowledge. To give account managers more time to manage the client relationship, we have been stepping up automation of fixed rate capital finance products, commercial mortgages and commercial instalment loans and leases. And we have taken steps to ensure greater account management continuity at our branches.

Commercial bankers concentrated on enhancing their account management skills and product knowledge, while better systems allowed them more time to work directly with clients.

Commercial Banking Centres

Given the special needs of commercial customers, the Bank has concentrated its commercial expertise in central locations at specialized branches known as Commercial Banking Centres. TD now has 98 centres located across the country, serving a high percentage of our business customers.

Industry Specialization

Knowing more about the customer's industry, competition and special market conditions gives our bankers an edge in meeting customers' needs. At the same time, it enables the Bank to design and implement useful and appropriate new services and products. TD has developed particular expertise in five key industry segments: agriculture, auto parts, communications, franchising, and health care.

Money Monitor

In response to the growing demand from our customers for immediate access to up-to-the-minute account information, TD is establishing links, through personal computer systems, to bring banking directly into the customer's office. To this end, we have developed a number of products including *Money Monitor*, which provides secure and immediate account access to commercial customers through their personal computers. By reducing the time Bank staff spend supplying such information, this product effectively increases the time available for customer service.

Payroll Products

The Bank's new payroll product, which enhances existing cash management services, has been very well received. The Bank now processes payrolls for more than 5,000 companies paying close to half a million Canadians. *Paymet*, the new payroll service launched last year, allows customers to access their own payroll data through a personal computer.

Facilitrade

As links with customers' computers have increased, TD has extended these networks to cover a broader range of banking services. *Facilitrade* is TD's automated system which allows customers to open letters of credit and receive reports through personal computers and transmit them to the Bank for processing. *Facilitrade* saves time and ensures accuracy for customers who issue a large volume of letters of credit.

Commercial banking activities 1987

	100%	Percentage of total number of commercial borrowers by size of authorized credit.	Percentage of total commercial loans outstanding by size of authorized credit.
	80		
	60		
	40		
■ Under $200,000		84.1%	25.3%
■ $200,000 to $5,000,000		15.1	53.7
■ Over $5,000,000	20	0.8	21.0

Ardèn Dervishian, owner of Boutique Ardème (left), and Yves Bergeron, Account Manager at TD's Commercial Banking Centre in Laval, Quebec, have worked closely together as Boutique Ardème has grown from a single costume jewelry shop to over 45 outlets in Ontario and Quebec.

An unorthodox graphic approach creates reader involvement in this bank report. Photographs, illustrations, and trap varnishes are all fitted dot-to-dot.

"Color separation was critical," Eskind reports. "The photographs were reproduced as four-color black-and-white. The illustrations were separated as four-color achromatic process, with dot-to-dot fitting of illustration to photo." Trap varnishes were likewise fitted dot-to-dot.

Considering what the art director calls the client's "tightly managed budget control," this report would seem an ambitious production. "Production is tightly managed to control costs," she says; "there's no press overtime, which is rather unheard of in this industry."

Still, the designers were not deterred. They segmented various printing forms to maximize economy, putting five colors plus a somewhat whimsical, speckly-looking tinted varnish on dull coated stock for the operations section. These pages were also garnished with simple vertical bar charts in bright colors. In the financial section, which sported the same speckled pattern in the margins, two or five colors were used variously to produce related brightly-colored, mostly horizontal graphs.

Report: Toronto-Dominion Bank 1987. Domestic and international banking. 1987 total assets $54.5 billion (Canadian).
Design firm: Eskind Waddell, Toronto, Ontario, Canada
Art director: Roslyn Eskind
Designers: Peter Scott, Glenda Rissman
Photographer: Bernard Bohn
Illustrator: Jeff Jackson
Copywriter: Toronto-Dominion Bank
Printer: Arthurs-Jones Lithographing Ltd., Mississanga, Ontario
Size: 8¼" by 11¾"; 80 pages plus covers
Quantity: 80,000 English; 6000 French; 3000 Japanese

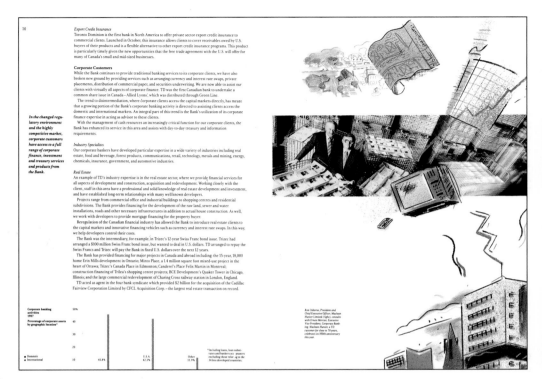

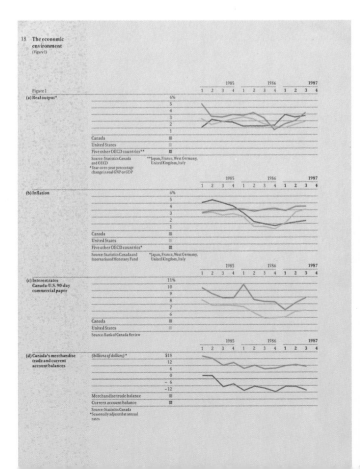

Drexel Burnham Lambert

It hadn't been an easy year for Drexel Burnham Lambert (DBL). Although the company had been considered *the* leading banking and securities firm, DBL's reputation had been rocked when three of its employees were implicated and then charged in a massive insider-trading scandal. Wisely, the chairman and CEO, Robert E. Linton and Frederick H. Joseph, respectively, addressed this problem directly in the first few paragraphs of DBL's 1986 annual report, and then went on to reassure DBL clients and observers: "Drexel Burnham adheres to the highest standards of conduct in its business dealings, and we believe our exemplary record is largely responsible for our continued success during this difficult period."

DBL's 1986 report bears out management claims. The company remained the number-one lead underwriter of high-yield corporate securities, topped the competition in preferred stock offerings and financing for industrial companies, and placed second in initial public offerings and private-placement volume. Indeed, if it hadn't been an easy year for DBL, it had certainly been a good one.

Essentially, DBL's 1986 report is a celebration of the company's ability to weather all sorts of change. "Drexel Burnham specializes in innovative financing," notes Michael Gericke, the Pentagram (New York) designer responsible for the report. "The company is at the forefront of interpreting and reacting to change. Historically, change has been met with

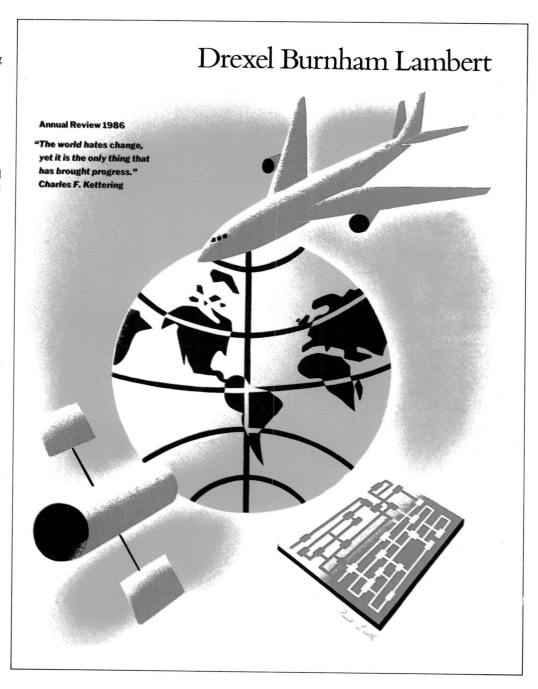

Drexel Burnham Lambert

Annual Review 1986

"The world hates change, yet it is the only thing that has brought progress."
Charles F. Kettering

resistance, but Drexel Burnham sees it as necessary to ensure America's economic health and position in the global marketplace."

Editorially, the report has been divided into discrete sections. Three of these, the management letter, the year-in-review (which includes financial statements), and an essay-cum-operations report titled "Helping People Manage Change," have been presented simply, in large type with marginal line illustrations, on a gray flannel text sheet. Not coincidentally, the DBL essay follows another, more far-reaching text entitled "The Changing Economy: Evolution in Perspective." This attempts to present a historical overview of America's evolving economy, with an eye toward significant innovations of the last 25 years, and it is this larger essay that becomes the visual and verbal heart of the report.

Curiously, the designers chose a group of European illustrators to visualize copy points in this section, for no reason, says Gericke, than that, of the American illustrators he looked at, "there were too many whose work had been seen, whereas the European illustrators were not as well known, and their work wasn't quite as predictable." Pentagram's London office was helpful here, both in collecting illustrators' work samples and in coordinating delivery of finished artwork. During the process, 14 illustrators were sent a quote from the essay as well as a brief provided by the client concerning the particular point they wanted that part of the essay to make. The

The Changing Economy: Evolution in Perspective

During World War II, American productivity and industrial ingenuity were the marvels of the world, and our country was the undisputed industrial leader. At that time Joseph Schumpeter, one of the most influential economists of this century, wrote about how important entrepreneurship is to American industry. While Schumpeter was impressed by the innovative abilities demonstrated by American entrepreneurs, he feared that the qualities that had made America the leader in the Industrial Revolution would wither unless the economic environment continued to encourage their activities.

Schumpeter wrote of the need for entrepreneurs to regularly engage in what he called "creative destruction," meaning a willingness to discard outworn methods, products, processes, ideas and strategies and replace them with new ones more appropriate to the times. Those who did so would prosper; the others would fall by the wayside.

In the past 25 years, corporations have faced increasing pressure from both domestic and foreign competitors as they struggle to improve quality, increase productivity and lower their labor and capital costs. In many manufacturing and service areas, America is losing its market dominance to Europe and the Far East. Productivity gains throughout the Pacific Rim have surpassed those in the United States. And businessmen and legislators are increasingly concerned about our nation's growing trade deficit.

To stay globally competitive, America must pursue an aggressive course in its government policies, economic decision making and international trade agreements. Yet the ultimate responsibility for America's competitiveness does not lie with the government, but with the corporations themselves. Their ability to respond to changes in technology, consumer preferences and international trade will determine their place in world markets. Those companies with the foresight to anticipate trends and the financial flexibility to capitalize on them will continue to prosper and grow. Companies that are slow to adjust or unable to respond may be absorbed by their competitors or simply fade into obscurity. While there are no easy solutions to America's competitive challenge, one thing is certainly clear: The strength of our economy depends on how well our corporations manage change, how effectively they can engage in Schumpeter's "creative destruction."

Throughout history, American entrepreneurs have shown a remarkable ability to adapt and respond. With a single-minded focus on profit and growth, they've overcome structural, technical

"We must live in a moment of history where change is so speeded up that we begin to see the present only when it is already disappearing." R.D. Laing

The success of American business and industry has always depended on our ability to manage change. In the face of stiff international competition and rapidly evolving markets, many corporations are returning to the entrepreneurial values and profit incentives that built their companies and our nation's economy in the process. At Drexel Burnham, we're helping our clients remain vital and competitive with innovative securities, strategic transactions and efficient market access to lower their cost of capital.

4

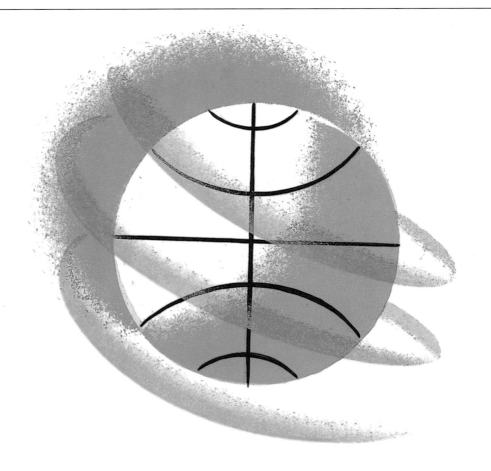

greater number of artworks commissioned, over those actually used, ensured that Gericke's long-distance designing would not go too far awry. Roughs were sent across the Atlantic via electronic facsimile, and in the end, the client and designer both selected which 10 of the 14 works were actually used.

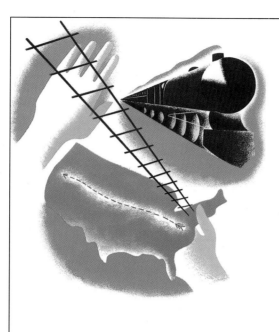

The Railways and the Road to Prosperity

In 1830, there were only 23 miles of operating railways in the U.S.; by the 1850s there were more than 30,000 miles of track connecting America's growing cities. The railroad industry quickly became the nation's most important and profitable enterprise – by 1855, U.S. investment in railroads had exceeded $300 million. Despite resistance from such notables as Martin Van Buren, who saw railroads forcing canal workers into unemployment, the development of the railroad was as inevitable as the march of time.

Railroads were America's first big business, and they strongly influenced the way other industries would operate. The far-flung lines like the Pennsylvania and the New York Central could not be run by a single person operating out of a solitary office, as a cotton mill was run. Instead, railroad executives had to delegate responsibilities to individuals far from headquarters, to the point where the major lines had several levels of managers. Indeed, the very concept of middle management originated with the railroads.

Novel concepts in financing were also important to the success of the railroads. Prior to the emergence of big business, investors tended to be local businessmen who could see their money at work simply by walking to the mill. Not so owners of stock in railroads and later corporations that imitated the railroads' organization. Railroads might stretch hundreds, even thousands, of miles and large corporations did business in many locations. In time investors would often live far from the companies' operations. Although such investment is quite common today, it was fresh, novel, and to some, frightening in the 1840s and 1850s.

Moreover, never before had an industry required such large amounts of capital. The European markets were major contributors to the railroads' massive capital needs, and by 1853 an estimated $50 million in U.S. railroad bonds were held abroad. State governments also played a major role in financing the construction of railroads, sometimes by purchasing privately issued railroad securities or by guaranteeing payments of interest and principal on railroad bonds.

The Age of Great Entrepreneurs

Wherever the railroads went, they had a far-reaching effect on American life. The iron horse could transport people, machines, food and supplies and made America's great westward expansion possible. It played a decisive role in the Civil War, and an even greater role in the nation's economic growth. It provided a cost-effective way to ship raw materials to distant factories and enabled finished goods to be distributed farther and faster than ever before.

"The world hates change, yet it is the only thing that has brought progress."
Charles F. Kettering

As railroads raced to lay tracks across inland America, their organizational and financial needs permanently changed the structure of American business and the shape of our capital markets. Over the years, corporate needs have continued to revolutionize our markets and our economy. In the mid-1970s, the demand for cost-efficient capital led Drexel Burnham to open the public debt market to non-investment grade issuers. Today, the high yield bond market accounts for some 20 percent of all straight corporate debt issued in America.

9

After a difficult year, lighthearted illustrations and more serious business essays emphasize Drexel Burnham Lambert's ability to weather any storm.

Report: Drexel Burnham Lambert 1986. Investment banking and related services. 1986 total assets $38.6 billion.
Design firm: Pentagram Design, New York City
Art director: Colin Forbes
Designer: Michael Gericke
Photographer: Neil Selkirk
Illustrators: Paul Leith, Irene Von Treskow, Su Huntley and Donna Muir, Simon Stern, Ian Beck, George Hardie, Jonathan Field, Dan Fern, Mattew Bell (paintings); Ward Schumaker (line drawings)
Copywriter: Drexel Burnham Lambert
Printer: Lithographix, Los Angeles
Size: 9″ by 12″; 56 pages plus covers
Quantity: 100,000

"Innovators are inevitably controversial."
Eva Le Gallienne

As the capital markets have become more volatile and complex, Drexel Burnham has led the development of new financial instruments and financing techniques to meet the needs of issuers and investors. We tailor our securities to specific cash flow requirements and other needs, giving issuers greater flexibility and control over their cost of capital. Our innovative securities also provide investors with a wider range of alternatives, allowing them to achieve more specific risk and reward objectives.

surprisingly, shareholders are beginning to wonder whose interests management decisions are designed to represent. While managers have a responsibility to deliver value to shareholders, they may face tremendous conflicts of interest. In some cases, increasing the company's efficiency and obtaining the greatest possible value for shareholders may threaten managers' jobs or the programs they have worked to establish and maintain.

A widening gap between owners and managers can encourage practices that are not beneficial to the company. Far from working on performance incentives, many top managers vote to increase their salaries and benefits when their companies' profits are declining. Others may retain unproductive business units under the guise of "long-range planning," even if it would be more profitable in both the long and short run to sell the units and reinvest the proceeds.

One reason why American corporations have become sluggish and unresponsive may stem from their size and structure. In many cases, the management hierarchies that brought American business into the modern age have become so large, complex and redundant that managers find it difficult to identify and resolve basic operating snags and productivity problems. A *New York Times* study concluded that excessive corporate bureaucracy, popularly known as "corpocracy," accounts for some $862 billion in waste each year – or six times as much as the Grace Commission attributed to Federal bureaucratic waste.

Market Forces and the New Entrepreneurs

According to the economics of Adam Smith, when businesses and trade fall out of balance, the "invisible hand" of market forces will inevitably step in to correct the situation. Yet in today's fast-paced markets, fundamental market forces often react too slowly to prompt effective change in time.

Of course, the markets do penalize poor management in a number of ways. Slipping sales and reduced market share can force managers to take corrective action. If a company's revenues and profitability decline and equity prices fall, shareholders are likely to take their capital elsewhere, which can result in further declines in stock prices and an increase in capital costs. In addition, companies that do not adequately utilize and restructure their balance sheets, thus weakening equity prices, are now more likely than ever to face unsolicited bids for control.

A new breed of entrepreneur is emerging in today's marketplace. These innovators are looking at the American corporation from a new perspective. They're looking for ways to increase profits and

18

Burbank-Glendale-Pasadena Airport Authority

It's not often that a client asks a designer for an annual report that's "exciting" and "different," or specifically cites photography and financial reporting as two areas where the designer should feel free to "stretch." But those are precisely the words that designer Thomas Devine says his client, Deborah Cohen, public-information officer for the Burbank-Glendale-Pasadena Airport Authority ("the Authority"), used when she approached him about designing the Authority's 1987 annual report.

Early meetings with the client and photographer Scott Morgan, Devine reports, dealt with fiscal highlights and other information which the Authority wanted its report to convey. But it was Cohen's enthusiasm for the unconventional, and her stylistic suggestions, that ultimately sparked the solution for the report.

"I was shown an example of spot illustration," Devine recalls, "and though I felt the specific style wasn't a direction we wanted to pursue, the idea of illustration stayed with me."

Indeed, illustration proved integral in creating what the designer calls a "mystique" for the airport in this report. But photography was also a factor. "The photographer was given creative freedom to explore the airport and to make pictures that interested him," Devine says. "Our discussions were never specific as to what the photographs would show, but rather, were concerned with conveying a feeling through the images—to create a mystique instead of documenting a certain location." With their tight croppings, soft frames, and

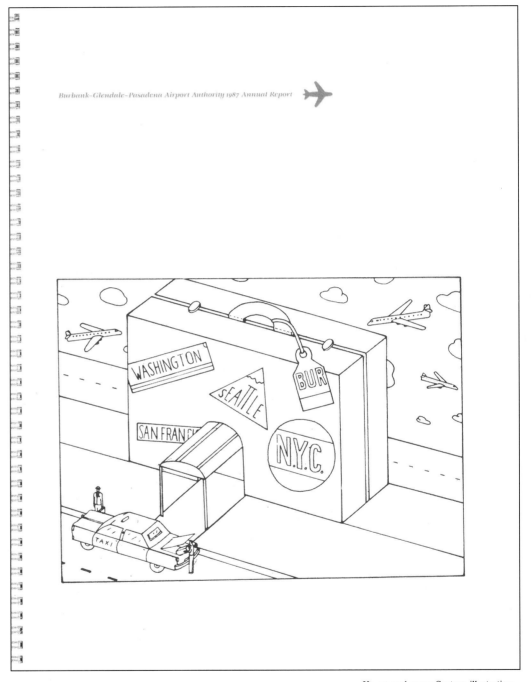

Burbank-Glendale-Pasadena Airport Authority 1987 Annual Report

Up, up and away: Cartoon illustrations and sprightly little airplanes work with impressionistic photography to describe a regional airport's pleasure in its own performance.

controlled use of double imagery and multiple exposure, Morgan's black-and-white photos do just that.

It was in depicting less visually interesting aspects of the airport that illustration played a key role, but, unlike his camera-toting counterpart, Stephen Turk was assigned specific subjects to draw. But even with his loose, cartoon style, Devine reports that Turk's initial attempts were a bit too safe. "I had to push him a bit to do things that he wouldn't usually be able to sell to a client," Devine says. "He had creative freedom; he just had to take advantage of it." Printed in dark gray on text leaves that intervene with glossy sheets imprinted with Morgan's unusual photography, Turk's whimsical drawings humorously highlight various of the Authority's progress points made during the year.

In addition, one of the cartoons opens the financial section, which was originally conceived as a separate book. The two reports were consolidated at the request of the client, who, Devine says, "felt that the financial book looked too nice. They were afraid that the airport commissioners would in the future want only a 'nice' financial book."

An additional note of whimsy is injected through the use of an airplane motif that recurs throughout the report. In the operations pages, it appears in a rich orange appropriately sunny for a Southern California airport and seems, like some impeccable skywriter, to pull a matching orange headline across the page. Opposite the

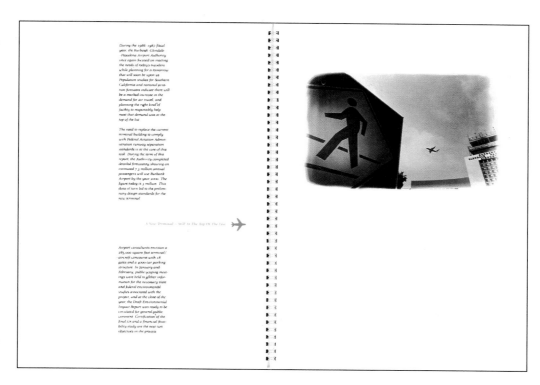

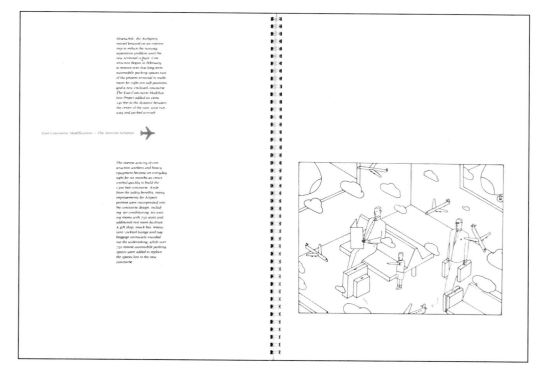

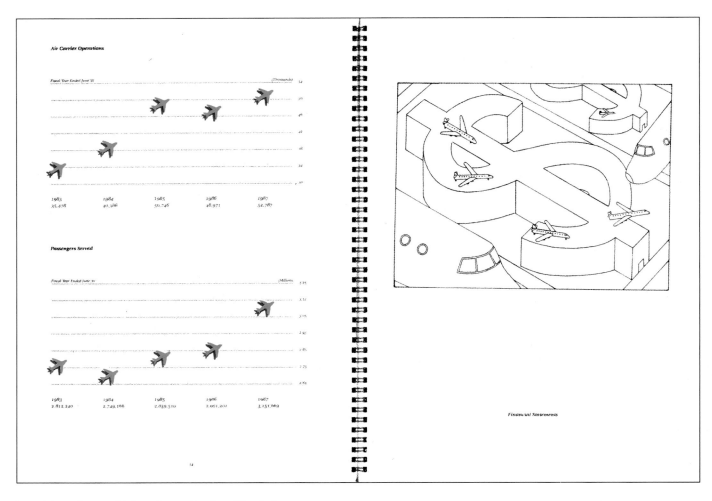

Air Carrier Operations

Fiscal Year Ended June '87 (Thousands)

1983	1984	1985	1986	1987
35,478	40,386	50,748	48,971	52,787

Passengers Served

Fiscal Year Ended June '87 (Millions)

1983	1984	1985	1986	1987
2,812,240	2,749,166	2,859,510	2,961,201	3,151,669

Financial Statements

financial section, multiples of this symbol plot graphs that show growth in air-carrier operations and the number of passengers served by the airport in the last five years.

The positioning of these little symbols elicited the only client-requested alteration in the report. "Originally," says Devine, "the little orange planes that 'pull' the type were pointed in many different directions and more specifically up and down. Management asked that I point them in any direction but down—they didn't want the positioning of the planes to convey the idea of crashing."

Looking Ahead — Taking Care Of Tomorrow's Needs

Report: Burbank-Glendale-Pasadena Airport Authority 1987. Public air terminal. 1987 total assets $90.7 million; 1987 income $2.68 million.
Design firm: Devine Design, Burbank, CA
Art director/designer: Thomas Devine
Photographer: Scott Morgan
Illustrator: Stephen Turk
Copywriters: Victor Gill, Deborah Cohen/Burbank Airport
Printer: Lithographix, Los Angeles
Size: 8⁵⁄₁₆″ by 11⁵⁄₈″; 32 pages including self-cover
Quantity: 2000

Modulaire

Despite record revenues in 1986, Modulaire, a San Francisco-based manufacturer and marketer of non-residential modular structures, had a disappointing bottom line. "There were a lot of factors influencing the company's performance that year," observes Steven Tolleson of San Francisco's Tolleson Design, who produced this report, "and the report was designed to address the eight or 10 questions analysts were most often asking about Modulaire's performance, and about the industry."

The question-and-answer concept became the report's driving force, yet the report's format is in no way bound by it. Rather than run the copy as a conventional string of "Q's" and "A's," the business report, which is untitled and has been signed by the chairman and the president, looks fairly like a straight operations review. The questions have been placed unobtrusively in the wide margin created by the report's horizontal orientation, and are keyed with a lower-case q printed in red. The answers, over in the running copy, have been similarly keyed by the letter a, set close to the appropriate paragraph.

It's to the designer's credit that the Q&A format did not interfere with the larger message of the report—showing Modulaire as a strong company with its problems well in hand. Every element in the report—the speckled brown, kraft-like paper for text sections, the caterpillar-yellow fly and divider pages, the three-dimensional-looking folios and graphs drawn to resemble brick

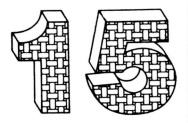

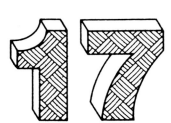

Financial Highlights

	1986	1985	1984
Total Revenues	$60,596,816	$48,189,671	$39,308,406
Gross Profits	20,741,589	19,117,877	16,282,996
Earnings Before Taxes on Income	2,191,801	4,387,616	3,221,947
Net Earnings	831,901	3,000,716	2,069,947
Net Earnings Per Share	0.28	1.09	0.93
Shares Outstanding	2,992,545	2,993,635	2,222,000

Profile
Modulaire Industries
rents, sells, services
and manufactures non-
residential, relocatable
modular structures.
These building systems,
ranging from single
mobile offices to multi-
module and multi-story
buildings, provide space
solutions for various markets including education,
construction, industry,
government and military.

Total Gross Revenues
by Market

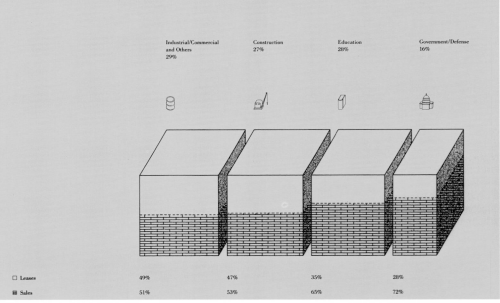

Industrial/Commercial and Others 29%	Construction 27%	Education 28%	Government/Defense 16%
☐ Leases			
49%	47%	35%	28%
▦ Sales			
51%	53%	65%	72%

*Kraft and coated papers ground both
photography and illustration in a
construction company report, where color
is used as a graphic effect. Page numbers,
shown enlarged at left, are given delightful
dimension and individuality.*

walls, stacks of modules, or opened metal tape rules—works in concert. "This is a construction company, a builder and manufacturer," says Tolleson, "and we wanted it to be perceived as such."

Photography, which, like the yellow pages, has been printed on a form of coated stock accommodated by a double saddle-wire binding, is in black-and-white. "There was no budget for photography," Tolleson says, "and the photos weren't art-directed." Instead, he told photographer Henrik Kam what he wanted and sent him alone to the company's Utah factory to get the major pictures. Other, pick-up shots came from the client's files and were run very small.

Besides easing budget restraints, the black-and-white imagery was also deemed appropriate to both Modulaire's business and its results that year. "Any time you photograph a factory in color," Tolleson explains, "you have so many factors in the environment working against you. Black-and-white photography minimizes that concern. And in this instance, the client didn't want the report to look expensive." The site photography was laser-scanned and printed in a duotone of black and gray for a rich, strong effect.

Report: Modulaire Industries 1986. Non-residential modular structures manufacture, marketing, and leasing. 1986 revenues $60.6 million.
Design firm: Tolleson Design, San Francisco
Art director/designer: Steven Tolleson
Photographer: Henrik Kam
Illustrators: Steven Tolleson, Nancy Paynter
Copywriter: Alvin Jacobsen/Modulaire
Printer: Graphic Arts Center, Portland, OR
Size: 11¾" by 8¾"; 28 pages plus covers
Quantity: 5000

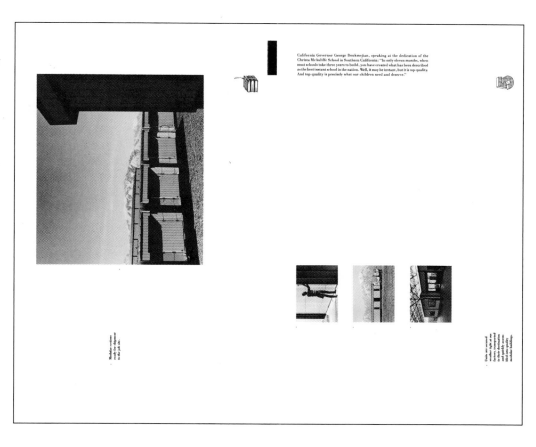

California Governor George Deukmejian, speaking at the dedication of the Christa McAuliffe School in Southern California: "In only eleven months, when most schools take three years to build, you have created what has been described as the best instant school in the nation. Well, it may be instant, but it is top quality. And top quality is precisely what our children need and deserve."

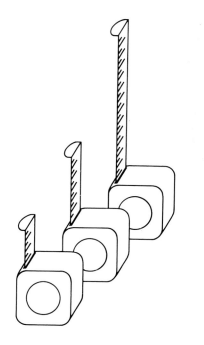

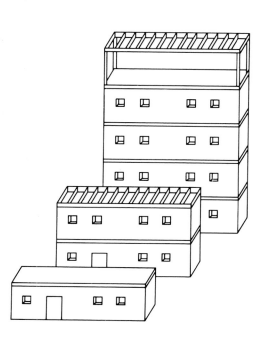

EnergyNorth

EnergyNorth is a small natural-gas utililty in southern New Hampshire. Since the area is one of the most rapidly growing parts of New England, it is an especially good market for an energy company.

When designers Michael Weymouth and José Lizardo, of Weymouth Design in Boston, first met with EnergyNorth's Michael Mancini and Michael Netkovick to discuss the 1987 annual report—the sixth which the design firm has produced for this client—they brought with them three separate and unique proposals. The first presented a collection of recipes from customers who cook with natural gas. The second was a series of seasonal photographs highlighting copy that would talk about how EnergyNorth's services change throughout the year. The third solution, the one ultimately accepted by management, documented the utility's growing customer base in a series of photo-collages.

"The objective of this solution was simple," says Weymouth. "Drawing from its customer base, the company created a pastiche of economic success stories, so that the reader would conclude that EnergyNorth's future is bright because its customers are doing so well."

Because the client's budget was limited, the designers planned the book's production very carefully. "Our intention," says Weymouth, "was to design it so it could be efficiently and economically produced at the printer's. Normally, we would use Scitex to assemble these kinds of images, but there was no budget for it. So we kept all of the production to straight-

ENERGYNORTH, INC.   ANNUAL REPORT 1987

KATHY

by 10.771 MCFD. Subject to FERC approval, partial deliveries may be available in November, 1988 with the
remaining supply available a year later.

Gas Prices

The price of gas declined in 1987 as a result of purchasing lower-priced gas supplies from independent
producers. Those purchases were the result of new federal regulations that give local distribution companies
access to third party gas. Tennessee agreed to transport that gas as of last March and the Company moved
the maximum volumes allowed. The Company is pleased with Tennessee's efforts to obtain and secure
reasonably priced sources of gas.

Falling prices for interruptible gas made it more competitive with residual oil and brought back many large
industrial customers with dual fuel capability. Interruptible sales more than doubled to 650,000 MCF, near
the levels prior to 1986. The margin earned on these sales, approximately $500,000 during 1987, is used
as a credit to firm customers through the cost of gas adjustment and serves to keep our rates
competitive.

Rates and Regulation

Obtaining rate relief was a high priority in fiscal 1987. All three utility subsidiaries received rate orders
from the New Hampshire Public Utilities Commission, concluding a period of intense activity. The full
impact of the rate increases is not yet apparent since not all were in effect for the entire fiscal year.

The new permanent increases have improved earnings, though regulatory lag remains a concern.
Historical ratemaking practices do not favor a fast-growing market because of the delay between the
time an investment is made and its incorporation in rates charged to customers; hence, the need for
more frequent rate filings to translate customer growth into earnings growth.

Gas Service, Inc. reached a final settlement with the Commission in March, 1987 providing for an
annual increase in base rates of $451,000. The settlement also allowed the Company to institute
thermal or heat content billing, which is expected to yield $136,000 in additional revenues.
Because the total increase of $587,000 was less than the temporary rates in effect since April,
1986, a refund is being made to customers through May, 1988. The refund liability was recorded
in 1987.

Late in the fiscal year, Concord Natural Gas Corporation and Manchester Gas Company were
granted annual rate increases of $394,000 and $481,000, respectively, both retroactive to
March, 1987. In these cases the final amounts allowed were greater than temporary rates in
effect during the period. This resulted in a deficiency to be recovered from customers over a
one-year period beginning November 1, 1987. The recoverable amounts were recorded as
income in fiscal 1987.

The Company was disappointed in the loss of its appeal to the New Hampshire Supreme
Court of an August, 1986 Commission decision in a prior Manchester Gas rate case. At issue
among other things was an allowance for attrition. Attrition is the eroding effect that
increased costs exert over time on a utility's rate of return in the face of fixed rates for its
services. The Court upheld the Commission's denial of an attrition allowance.

8

EnergyNorth's natural gas
and propane service area
has seen a boom in the
manufacturing sector and
the expansion of our higher
education institutions.
Leaders in business and
education continue to work
together to develop a
highly-skilled and reliable
work force.

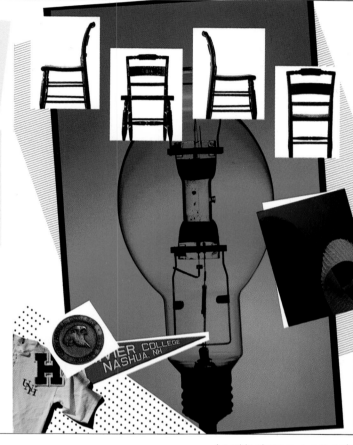

*A pastiche of company success stories
gains momentum with photomontage.*

edge stripping or knock-out white backgrounds, and we ganged the separations."

The designers also took advantage of their firm's considerable photographic capabilities to produce all of the images in-house. "We got all the props together and shot it in about four days," Weymouth says. "Larry Long did the shooting, and being a designer, he understood the potential production problems as well as anybody."

To facilitate stripping, many of the still-lifes were photographed against a background of square ceramic tiles, or reproduced with the chrome's black border intact. Even irregularly shaped silhouetted objects were inset in angular knock-outs, and right-angled patterns of dots and rules, which were handled much like the photo elements, helped to unify the overlaying shapes.

Finally, a double saddle-wire binding allowed the four-color process to be printed on a single four-page form of high-gloss paper, which was interleaved with eight pages of the less expensive dull-coated stock used for the rest of the book. This invention effectively spread the four-color imagery through a larger part of the report, which was too small to perfect bind. One or two colors only were used on the remaining pages. "By printing fewer colors on the majority of the paper," Lizardo notes, "we were able to produce a color report for less money." Typeface throughout was Gill Sans Light Italic, he adds, because "the design solution called for a contemporary-looking face."

Report: EnergyNorth, Inc. Natural gas distribution. 1987 revenues $64.5 million.
Design firm: Weymouth Design, Boston, MA
Art director: Michael Weymouth
Designer: José Lizardo
Photographers: Larry Long, Michael Weymouth
Copywriters: Carolyn Disco, Michael Netkovick/EnergyNorth
Printer: Acme Printing, Wilmington, MA
Size: 8½″ by 11″; 28 pages plus covers
Quantity: 5500

Photography was done by the designers and stripped together in angled cuts to curtail production costs.

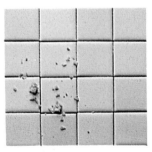

Immunex

Immunex Corporation is an emerging biotechnology company whose business, as its name suggests, centers around therapies related to malfunctions of the immune system. Like other pharmaceutical companies, Immunex must spend long years in research and development before a new drug can be brought to clinical trials.

With particular emphasis on the clinical trial phases, Immunex's 1987 report—designed by Pentagram (San Francisco)—both reviews the company's current operations and research and explains the years spent in development. At the center of this explanation—and of the report itself—is a complex annotated illustration by Ed Lindlof. "This single illustration, spread across a double gatefold, allowed us to graphically visualize the complex and lengthy pharmaceutical/governmental process of bringing a product to market," says Pentagram's Kit Hinrichs.

But before they could explain the process to Immunex's audience of financial institutions and analysts, the designers—Hinrichs and associate Belle How—and the illustrator had to understand it themselves. Under direction from Stuart Parker, Immunex director of corporate communications, the client "walked through" the complicated pharmaceutical and governmental steps with Hinrichs and Lindlof. But it was the illustrator's efforts, Hinrichs notes, that really made a difference. "Ed was an invaluable resource in pulling this project together," he says. "He traveled from Austin,

IMMUNEX

1987 ANNUAL REPORT

Our manufacturing capabilities will become reality with the spring 1988 completion of a pilot-scale fermentation plant, a major asset of Immunology Ventures, our successful 50/50 joint venture with Eastman Kodak Company. Immunology Ventures was formed in 1986 to develop and manufacture certain lymphokine therapeutic products. The pilot plant, located at Immunex's headquarters in downtown Seattle, is designed to meet Good Manufacturing Practices requirements as established by the FDA and has the capacity to manufacture products for both clinical trials and commercial sale.

During the last year, while work in the production plant has been left primarily to workers with hardhats and drills, our manufacturing needs have been met by extraordinary efforts of the scientific staff. Using equipment intended for production of experimental amounts of our products, the staff produced sufficient quantities of GM-CSF, G-CSF, IL-3, IL-1, and IL-4 for clinical testing.

This production work, which often required extended periods of 'round-the-clock attention, was accomplished in addition to Immunex's continuing and substantial scientific progress.

In 1987, Immunex researchers were the first to clone genes encoding human Interleukin-7 and the Interleukin-1 receptor. Patent applications have been filed to protect these discoveries, and scientific papers have been submitted for publication. We are excited about these developments, but have withheld detailed public disclosure to permit peer review and publication prior to public discussion of these achievements. Additional information concerning these proteins and their potential therapeutic applications will be included in upcoming quarterly reports to our shareholders.

Our screening lab, which uses proprietary techniques to screen Eastman Kodak's library of organic compounds, has also met with success. Our efforts to identify organic molecules that mimic or block immune system activities have produced two "hits." We have identified classes of compounds which help predict the structure of second and third generation products, including potential therapeutics in the area of allergies. These organic compounds could have even greater market potential than recombinant protein products because it might be possible to give them orally rather than via injection.

STEPHEN A. DUZAN
President and CEO

Details of these and other significant accomplishments are included in the Operations Review, which begins on page six of this report. In connection with this review, we've invited several investment analysts to ask questions which they would like us to address. These questions, and our answers, appear within the same pages.

Planning for our future, we have continued to invest in research in new technologies. In addition to screening organic compounds, we are following promising avenues in the areas of transgenics, oncogenes, and protease inhibitors, and we maintain an active interest in developing the possibilities of rational drug design.

The composition of Immunex's Board of Directors changed over the year with the retirement of one of our board members and the addition of a new director. We extend our thanks and appreciation for the guidance given to us by Martin S. Gerstel, president of Alza Corporation, who stepped down from the Board in May. And we welcome Kirby L. Cramer, Ph.D., chairman of Hazleton Laboratories and Kirschner Medical Corporation.

1987 was an exciting year for Immunex. Our expectations for the year ahead are equally high.

STEVEN GILLIS, CHRISTOPHER S. HENNEY
Executive Vice Presidents

We will have more products in clinical trials than ever before and will be playing a greater role in managing the trial process. At the same time, we are continuing to develop new research opportunities for future product development.

During this period of growth, we share stockholder concerns that current stock prices don't reflect an appropriate value for the company and we are mindful of the scarcity of additional new capital for emerging firms. Our plans are based on the assumption that the market will not recover soon, and our objectives are balanced with the need to carefully marshal our financial resources.

A final challenge to be met in the coming year is a challenge to our management of Immunex's internal culture. As we add new functions and make the transition to a larger, more versatile company, we must continue to nurture the energy and enthusiasm of the scientists who take the lead with cutting edge research. It is upon their discoveries that Immunex will build its future as an independent pharmaceutical company.

Stephen A. Duzan
President

Texas, to Seattle to meet with Immunex scientists and researchers. In addition, he did significant independent research to augment the Immunex data."

The product of Lindlof's copious research is a pen-and-ink landscape inhabited by the various accouterments of biotech research. Here and there, a human hand holds a laboratory dish, a stethoscope, or a vial, reminding us that, after all, all of this science and research, the stacks of test results and trial data, is a human process, too, aimed at saving human lives. The large horizontal drawing is tied to the cover with a smaller drawing that also involves human hands, and with a soft, "healing" green color that forms a backdrop for the cover art and wraps around the outside of the gatefold. More small drawings, printed in matched colors, run through a question-and-answer operations review.

Accompanying the gatefold illustration are head shots of Immunex doctors, researchers, and managers, and an easy-to-read text that leads the reader through the drug development process. The text and photos

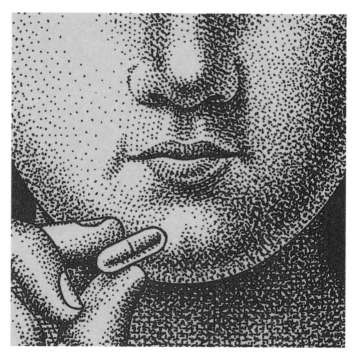

With a double gatefold illustration, this report explains the long and arduous process of bringing a bio-tech product to market. Other, smaller drawings highlight a question-and-answer business review.

are printed in the same strong colors as those used for copy and art on the operations review spreads. "We thought the illustrations should be in one color," says Hinrichs, "in order to retain their no-nonsense, pharmaceutically credible look. So we developed a special set of matched inks in which to reproduce the type, photos and smaller drawings."

Report: Immunex Corporation 1987. Biotechnology. 1987 revenues $15.7 million.
Design firm: Pentagram Design, San Francisco
Art director: Kit Hinrichs
Designers: Kit Hinrichs, Belle How
Photographer: Steve Firebaugh
Illustrator: Ed Lindlof
Copywriter: Katie Weiss
Printer: Graphic Arts Center, San Francisco
Size: 7¾" by 12"; 28 pages plus covers
Quantity: 20,000

Caremark

In 1986, Caremark had a happy story to tell. It had tallied record revenues and earnings, and had been recognized by Inc. magazine as one of the fastest growing publicly-held companies in the U.S. for the third year in a row. One of the reasons for Caremark's success was the decline in hospitalization and its concomitant demand for high-technology care in the home—Caremark's core business. The company wanted to convey both of these ideas—its success, and its technology—in its 1986 annual report.

Organizationally, this report may seem a bit lopsided. Those who read reports are used to seeing the shareholder message and the operations section compressed into a few pages of text, so that the theme section can be spread lavishly across many pages. This book does just the opposite: it opens with a shareholder letter that is also an operations review; this text extends through the report's first 17 pages. The next three spreads create the theme section, and the financials fill the remainder of the book, or 14 pages.

"The client wanted a running letter," explains Jim Berté of Robert Miles Runyan & Associates in Playa del Rey, California, "with charts and graphs to highlight various points in the text. Originally, this section was to have even more charts, so that the layout was more a matter of orchestration than design. It had a particularly nice look, but as time went by, the client kept cutting the charts until only a few were left."

While the original intent had

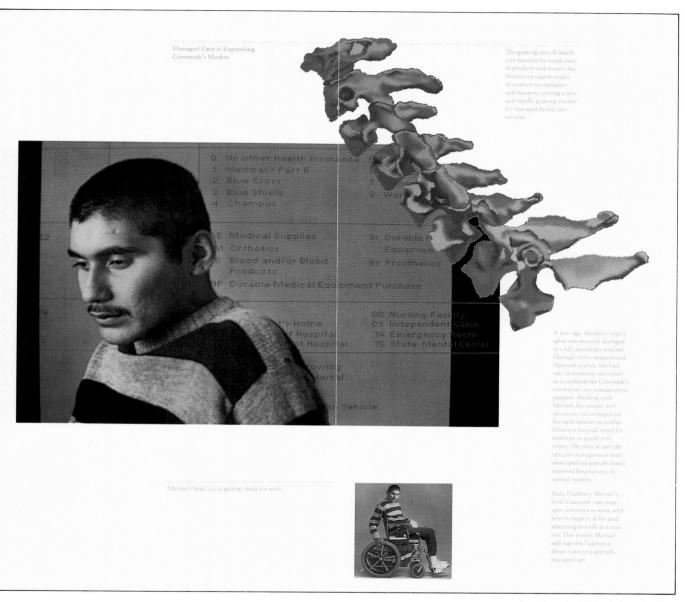

Managed Care is Expanding
Caremark's Market.

0 No other Health Insurance
1 Medical - Part B
2 Blue Cross
3 Blue Shield
4 Champus

6E Medical Supplies   9r Durable M
M Orthotics   Equipment
B Blood and/or Blood   9s Prosthetics
    Products
9P Durable Medical Equipment Purchase

                            08 Nursing Facility
      's Home   09 Independent Clinic
      t Hospital   14 Emergency Room
      t Hospital   15 State Mental Center

                    owing
                  ferral

              t Vehicle

A year ago Michael Orejel's
spine was severely damaged
in a fall; paraplegia resulted.
Through HRA's computerized
Optimed system, Michael
was immediately identified
as a candidate for Caremark's
innovative case management
program. Working with
Michael, his insurer and
physician, HRA arranged for
his rapid transfer to a rehabilitation hospital noted for
expertise in spinal cord
injury. The plan of care the
HRA case management team
developed reduced Michael's
expected hospital stay by
several months.

Kady Dunleavy, Michael's
local Caremark case man-
ager continues to work with
him in support of his goal:
returning to work as a cou-
rier. This month Michael
will take his California
driver's test in a specially
equipped van.

Michael Orejel, 23, is getting ready for work.

*A company specializing in home health
care describes its business in a series of
poignant case histories and a lengthy
letter-cum-operations review.*

been to place the charts and graphs in the text near the illustrated copy point, that became no longer possible. Instead, each graph was placed on the left-hand page of the spread, and, where possible, a dotted line was run from it to the appropriate copy block—a device that still serves to call out the pertinent area of text for the reader. The charts themselves were created out of a solid gray background using two additional PMS colors— fuschia and medium blue—plus black.

In the theme section, these same four colors were used to print the "high-tech" imagery describing Caremark's three areas of business expansion—managed care, new therapies, and biotechnology. Photographic portraits of Caremark patients, made by Deborah Meyer, were montaged in a computer with images associated with each case—a spinal X-ray for a man with a spinal injury, DNA strands for a child suffering from hypopituitary dwarfism, a

cardiogram for a man awaiting a heart transplant. By cropping and silhouetting around the images, Berté created a kind of spatial dynamic that enlivens each spread. Again, the running dots help draw the reader's eye to the particular message being illustrated.

Although Berté isn't quite satisfied with the color reproduction in this section— some of the subtler distinctions in the halftones, he feels, were lost in the separation—their mauve-y overtones create a seriousness befitting a company that deals in saving lives. And, since the colors themselves were drawn from Caremark's recently implemented corporate identity program, the palette also works to strengthen the company's emerging sense of style.

Report: Caremark, Inc. 1986. Home health-care management. 1986 revenues $135 million.
Design firm: Robert Miles Runyan & Associates, Playa dey Rey, CA
Art director/designer: Jim Berté
Photographer: Deborah Meyer
Copywriter: Larry Watts/Caremark
Printer: Lithographix, Los Angeles
Size: 7″ by 12″; 40 pages plus covers
Quantity: 25,000

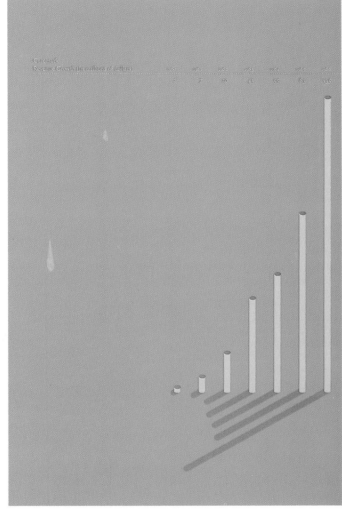

Complementing the text, full-page charts are built from the same matched colors used to reproduce the patient portraits.

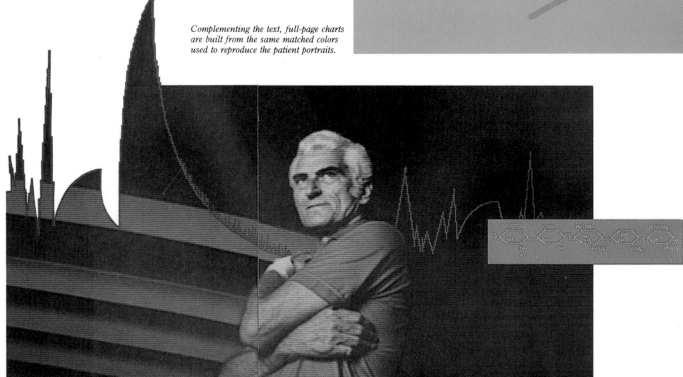

University of
Southern California

A leading private university with a national reputation, the University of Southern California is sometimes seen as a "rich kid's school," or as a football factory. But USC, in fact, attracts all types of students, from all economic levels, from all over the world. It considers its prime responsibility as preparing leadership for the 21st century, and this notion has been the focus of the university's fund-rasing campaign for the past four years.

In its own way, USC's 1987 financial report supports this theme of quality education, while at the same time addressing the concerns of parents and students about rising tuition costs. It is a thoughtful blend of essay and portraiture, couched in a restrained but subtly luxurious presentation that somehow manages to give both verbal and visual segments equal, but very different, weight.

This was the first USC report produced by the Morava & Oliver Design Office in Santa Monica, California, and its early development included laying the groundwork for the client/designer relationship. Designer Douglas Oliver reports that the client representatives, senior vice-president for administration Lyn Hutton and her assistant, Kathy Long-Phinney, "[were] as organized and as responsive as any corporate client. They had chosen the theme themselves and, after discussion with us, selected the students to be photographed."

Since the student portraits were to carry half of the report's message, it was

University of Southern California   1987 Financial Report

"All who have meditated on the art of governing mankind have been convinced that the fate of empires depends on the education of youth" ARISTOTLE (384-322 BC)

necessary that the subjects be examples of the school's academic and personal excellence. Thus, all of the students selected were "stars" in at least two areas—academics, sports, student government, social commitment, etc.—and represented the school's full range of cultural and ethnic diversity. Moreover, since the book had to be delivered on October 1, 1987, and had a six-month production schedule, it was necessary to make the portraits five months in advance, before the students left the campus for their summer vacations.

Executed in a piercing, forthright, yet appealing style, the portraits, which sandwich an essay illuminating the evolution and composition of USC's student body, are printed as black-and-white duotones. Their quiet strength extends directly from the portrait of the school's president, which appears next to his message, and thoroughly dispels any doubts we might have had about USC's commitment to scholarship. That the students seem both serious and likable, and that they immediately convey the diversity of the USC student body, also reflects well on the school.

The text pages work as effectively, if with less panache, as the portrait sections. Here, the mood is subdued and dignified, achieved with speckled ivory and buff text papers and matched inks. The essays are printed in two shades of brown, akin to sepia and sienna, and speak of wood-paneled libraries full of

James H. Zumberge
President

overstuffed leather chairs. Not
that they are stuffy themselves,
but rather, that the subject—
the education of youth—is
a matter for serious
consideration, by intelligent
men and women.

Perhaps the words of
Aristotle, which appear on the
report's cover, really do say it
best: "All who have meditated
on the art of governing mankind
have been convinced that the
fate of empires depends on the
education of youth." It is to that
conviction that this report
would seem to be dedicated.

*Student portraits confirm a university's
role in preparing the leadership of
tomorrow.*

Report: University of Southern
California 1987. Higher education.
1987 total assets $1.1 billion.
Design firm: Morava & Oliver Design
Office, Santa Monica, CA
Art director/designer: Douglas
Oliver
Photographer: Eric Myer
Copywriters: Lyn Hutton, Kathy
Long-Phinney/USC
Printer: Anderson Lithograph, Los
Angeles
Size: 8½" by 11"; 54 pages plus covers
Quantity: 25,000

Hasbro

Hasbro's 1986 annual report is a celebration of Hasbro's leadership position in the toy and game industry. But it's also a bit of a game in itself.

With some of the most popular toys and games in the world, Hasbro, Inc., is the largest and most diversified company in its industry. In addition to its well-known line of Hasbro toys, the company also produces and markets Milton Bradley games and puzzles, as well as the Playskool line of "educational" toys. Its products appeal to both children and adults, and it is this range of product and appeal, as well as its commitment to new products, that the company wanted to convey in its 1986 annual report.

When Pentagram designers Peter Harrison and Suzanne Morin first met with Hasbro's chairman and CEO, Stephen Hassenfeld, and vice-president for investor relations Robert Hubbell to discuss the report, they presented several ideas in rough concept form. These, Morin states, were narrowed down to the one the chairman felt best expressed the theme "The product is king." This concept involved showing Hasbro toys and games quite literally. However, aspects of other suggested alternatives, in particular a design approach that actively involved the reader, were adapted to the chosen format. "The company needed a more conservative approach, to reflect more quietly a year of slower growth," Morin says. "However, the spirit of visual games and quizzes remained in the final solution."

The visual focus of the report

HASBRO, INC. ANNUAL REPORT 1986

Gatefolds, which frame spread product-use photography, open to reveal reader-involving quizzes and games centered on Hasbro's own toys and games.

is the large and self-evident spread color photographs that alternate with the business review. In each, a group of children are seen playing in a room jammed with Hasbro products, from glamorous rock-star fashion dolls and fantastic animals with long, combable hair, to action-hero dolls, board games, and ingeniously designed robots and vehicles that can be transformed into one or more different toy configurations. The sheer number of toys, as well as their variety of design and multiplicity of color, first overwhelms report readers and then draws them in.

The "in" to which the reader is drawn is the area shaped by the short-paged, double gatefold into which the photographs have been placed. Inside these slightly-less-than-half-sheets are a series of quizzes designed to test the reader's Hasbro marketing savvy: Place a check next to the products you can locate (in the picture). Match the promotional phase to which each product belongs. What percentage of the company's revenues came from GI Joe last year? What was the company's biggest market outside the U.S. in 1986? The answers to these questions can be gleaned by

reading the copy on the outside of the gatefolds—or simply by turning to the answers, which have been printed inside the gatefolded back cover.

Despite the lush photography, six-color production, and gloss and dull varnishes over photos and text pages, respectively, the job was not without its economies. "The budget strongly affected design and production," Morin says. "Because of it, we had to reduce the number of photos we'd planned, and it precluded any location photography. The sets were re-used for the several different photos."

Much of this challenge, she adds, was met by the ingenuity of the photographer, Bruce Wolf, and his set-builder, Ron Focarino. "The style of photography was a crucial part of this assignment," Morin says, "and Bruce's input was of remarkable value. Both the photographer and the set designer were highly constructive in interpreting the designers' concept."

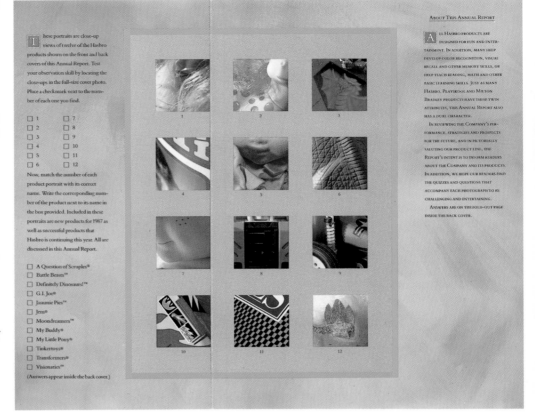

The fun begins with a photo quiz, placed inside the gatefolded front cover. Elsewhere, children's drawings highlight wide columns of text.

Report: Hasbro, Inc. 1986. Toy and game development, manufacture and marketing. 1986 revenues $1.3 billion.
Design firm: Pentagram Design, New York City
Art directors/designers: Peter Harrison, Suzanne Morin
Photographer: Bruce Wolf
Set builder: Ron Focarino
Copywriter: Robert Hubbell/Hasbro
Printer: Hennegan, Cincinnati, OH
Size: 9″ by 11¾″; 56 pages plus covers
Quantity: 50,000

Leaf

Few products are as much fun as gumballs and candy, and few can bring as much delight to young and old alike. Confectionary treats say "thank you" to a host, or "I love you" to a sweetheart, and spare the trick every Halloween. "Most of us," as Leaf, Inc.'s 1987 annual report points out, "regardless of our ages, our incomes, or our nationalities, use candy to make friends." And friends, old and new, are what this annual report is all about.

The best way to show our friends, of course, is to show pictures of them, and that is what this report does. But it is the manner of presentation that sets this book apart from being just another people book, for it combines black-and-white and color imagery within the same frame, and then puts it all together in a somewhat whacky layout.

Since each friend was to be shown with one of Leaf's products, which are sold under different names around the world, the challenge was how to keep the candy from being eclipsed by the larger presence in the photograph. Designer Greg Samata, of Samata Associates, in Dundee, Illinois, decided to highlight the products by reproducing them in color within otherwise black-and-white photographic portraits. "When you show a person with a product," says Samata, "the product gets quite small. We thought this technique would make the product stand out, as well as be more appealing and more fun."

The technique involved making two sets of black-and-white prints, one four times the

LEAF, INC. ANNUAL REPORT 1987

WE MAKE GOOD FRIENDS

In 1983, when Leaf, Inc. was formed by the acquisition of three existing candy and gum companies, we acquired some major opportunities and some major problems.

Included among our opportunities were several well-known and well-established brand names in the United States, Canada, and Europe, and many talented people with significant candy-industry experience.

Listed among our problems were an unmanageable network of more than 300 brokers, an inefficient and expensive distribution system, virtually no customer service organization, literally thousands of product items in our line and several products whose quality and marketing support had been allowed to deteriorate.

We spent the first three years of the company's life solving the problems we inherited. Our broker network is now one-tenth its former size. It includes 30 of the most effective brokers in the United States, all of whom work with Leaf more as a part of the company than as outside agents. Our distribution system has been streamlined, and now our customers may request immediate delivery of all of Leaf's products in a single shipment.

We have continued to cut the number of items in our line, allowing us to concentrate on our 15 leading brands and their most popular sizes and varieties. We have improved the quality of many of our brands, and have continued to increase our advertising and promotional expenditures significantly.

The year 1987, however, was the year to move ahead with building our brands—and we did so aggressively.

In 1987, combined sales of Leaf, Inc., Leaf Sweden and Leaf Finland reached $449 million. Of that, the operations of Leaf, Inc., not including Leaf Sweden and Leaf Finland, were $375 million, an increase of 18.3 percent over 1986. Net income for Leaf, Inc. was $7.2 million, up 25.5 percent over fiscal 1986.

In mid-November 1987, we acquired the trademarks of the former Chuckles Company, including Chuckles® jellied candies and Pine Bros® cough drops, two major brands in the northeastern United States. We are confident that the Chuckles and Pine Bros. brands have great potential for growth nationally.

In early January 1988, we acquired 49 percent of the outstanding shares in L. S. Heath & Sons, Inc., makers of the Heath English Toffee Bar and Heath ice cream product ingredients.

In 1987, Leaf assumed operational responsibility for the candy division of our parent company, Huhtamaki Oy, of Finland. The division, locally known as Hellas, is called Leaf Finland in the international marketplace. In addition, Leaf, Inc. assumed management of Kanolds, a Swedish candy manufacturer in which Huhtamaki, in 1987, acquired the 50 percent of the shares it did not own previously. Kanolds is now known as Leaf Sweden.

Net Sales
(in thousands)

87	$449,100	
86	$317,369	
85	$308,562	
84	$314,795	

Operating Income
(in thousands)

87	$ 37,900	
86	$ 22,982	
85	$ 19,319	
84	$ 13,553	

▫Leaf, Inc. ■Leaf Sweden and Leaf Finland

Erkki Railo, President and Chief Executive Officer, Leaf, Inc.

In 1987, two-thirds of the consolidated sales of Leaf, Inc., Leaf Sweden and Leaf Finland came from U.S. operations, while the remaining one-third resulted from operations overseas.

In 1988, Leaf, Inc. will pursue its long-term growth objectives by continuing to improve its products and plants, strengthen its marketing and promotional capabilities, and enhance its already excellent customer service system. We will continue to acquire compatible products with high-growth potential, and increase market share of our leading brands through broader geographic distribution.

size of the reproduction copy. Then, photo-retoucher George Sawa hand-colored the product portion of the print to the proper colors. The colored portion of the blow-up was then separated for color, reduced, and inset as a vignette in the black-and-white portrait. On press, the black plate was withheld in the area of the illustration, to give the product a more luminous appearance.

To further expand the "fun" aspect of both the products and the portraits, Samata incorporated them into an asymmetrical layout. Text columns have been set off one perpendicular edge at the left, with the right-hand edge dropping off at a slant. From this edge, one of the portraits, cropped to a dynamic trapezoid, has been set. Headlines and caption lines have been set

For confectioner Leaf, an unconventional format and combination photography say that, for people of all ages, candy is fun.

askew, as have various dot-patterned blips that hold the folios on the page. Finally, scattered across each spread are a range of Leaf products, reproduced in bright, if somewhat garish, solid shades that have been built up with big dots of process colors. The whole effect is not too distant from that of a gumball machine gone wild.

As the second Leaf report produced by Samata Associates, and infused with an exuberance similar to its predecessor's, the 1987 book again testifies to the willingness of corporate management—in this case, president and CEO Erkki Railo—to give the designers room to play (even though the previous year the Samatas photographed him in a sea of gumballs). "He trusts us to be professionals and to do what we do," Greg Samata says, "and he keeps his hands out. It's terrific."

And he gets his company a terrific report.

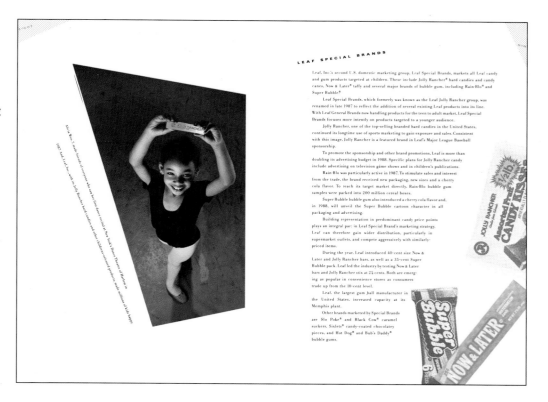

Report: Leaf, Inc. 1987. Confectionary products. 1987 sales $375 million.
Design firm: Samata Associates, Dundee, IL
Art director/designer: Greg Samata
Photographer: Mark Joseph
Illustrator: George Sawa (photo-retouching)
Copywriter: Joel Feldstein/N.W. Ayer
Printer: Great Northern Printing, Skokie, IL
Size: 8¼″ by 12″; 32 pages plus covers
Quantity: 10,000

In producing this annual report, designers at Pentagram's San Francisco office had two distinct challenges. The first—which comprised the theme of the report— was to introduce a new company that had been formed in 1986 by two of the oldest and most revered companies in the entertainment business. The second was to do it in only 10 weeks.

The first meeting with the client, reports Pentagram art director/designer Kit Hinrichs, was "absolute panic as to how we would be able to complete the report in the time allowed." Nonetheless, Hinrichs and colleague Karen Berndt came up with half a dozen alternatives from which MGM/UA could choose. A particular favorite was a view of the company seen through various well-known film props—Dorothy's ruby shoes from *The Wizard of Oz*, or Yul Brynner's six-gun from *The Magnificent Seven*.

But the approach chosen in the end lent particular strength to the new company: It combines the individual MGM/UA histories in a pictorial presentation that emphasizes the influential role both companies have played in the development of the film and entertainment business, and it brings their separate entities together under the copy line: "Two proud pasts. One glorious future."

Essential to the realization was locating the archival imagery needed to track the company time-line that ran through the theme section. The client's office of corporate communications, headed by vice-president Peter Graves, was actively involved in this

process. But, because of what Hinrichs characterizes as a somewhat ragged collection of photos in the client's library, the design team was forced to track down many of the earlier poster and promotional images from private collections, Hollywood poster shops, and the Academy of Motion Picture Arts and Sciences.

Another problem involved the use of historical images, some owned by the company and some the property of MGM's previous owner, Ted Turner. "At the time we were working on the report," Hinrich recalls, "there was a significant battle raging over the colorization of old movies that was being done by Ted Turner. We planned to use many hand-colored photos in the report, several of which were done in the 1930s and '40s. There were long discussions as to whether this implied MGM/UA was going to 'colorize' its own film library." In the end, several classic images, now owned by Turner, were eliminated altogether and the designers used the original hand-tinted prints, as planned.

Incredibly, the short production cycle did not deter the designers from commissioning a somewhat celebratory "movie poster" to run on the cover, as a divider page separating the historical section (up front) from the more conventionally presented shareholder letter and operations review, and as a full-size poster for shareholder distribution. More incredibly, the painting made it into the report, even though the artist, Doug Johnson, became ill during its last stages.

"Deadlines were so tight

Signing the United Artists Certificate of Incorporation in 1919 are (left to right) Douglas Fairbanks, Charlie Chaplin, D. W. Griffith (seated), Albert Banzhaf, Dennis F. O'Brien and Mary Pickford.

1920	1924	1924	1928	1929

United Artists' *The Son of the Sheik*, 1926

A single timeline fuses the past for two entertainment companies who recently joined forces.

In the early 1960s, many companies start to work with independent production companies in much the same way United Artists has from its inception.

Successful theatrical releases during the period are those that provide high quality entertainment—particularly those with action, adventure, intrigue, humor or compelling music.

United Artists' films, in particular, find an eager audience. Such classics as *The Magnificent Seven,* *Birdman of Alcatraz,* *Judgment at Nuremberg,* *Irma La Douce* and *West Side Story* are enormously successful.

United Artists also takes steps to become a major supplier of television productions in 1960, with the acquisition of Ziv Production Co. The company, creator of *Sea Hunt,* *The Outer Limits* and other popular television series, provides United Artists with a rapid expansion into the television market.

The Magnificent Seven, 1960

1960
United Artists acquires Ziv Productions, creators of many TV hits, including *Sea Hunt.*

1961
Burton Bacall Burt Lancaster wins a role of other stars stardom in *The Birdman of Alcatraz.*

1961
One of Burt Lancaster's greatest performances: *Birdman of Alcatraz.*

1962
King of rock and roll, Elvis Presley stars in *Kid Galahad.*

1962
Doctor No, the first of the enormously successful James Bond series, debuts.

1963
Irma La Douce teams Shirley MacLaine and Jack Lemmon again, this time in the apartment is in Paris.

1963
Steve McQueen, as a war prisoner, heads an all-star cast in *The Great Escape.*

20

21

that we had a stand-in cover and inside illustration," says Hinrichs, "just in case Doug couldn't complete it in time. But the artwork arrived at the printer about eight hours before it had to go on press. It was close, but we made it."

Report: MGM/UA 1986. Film and television entertainment. 1986 revenues $355 million.
Design firm: Pentagram Design, San Francisco
Art director: Kit Hinrichs
Designers: Kit Hinrichs, Karen Berndt
Photographers: Eric Myer, Terry Heffernan, Barry Robinson
Illustrators: Doug Johnson (major), Dave Stevenson
Copywriter: Burson & Marsteller
Printer: Anderson Lithograph, Los Angeles
Size: 7⅞" by 12"; 68 pages plus covers
Quantity: 30,000